VELVET

D1113287

VELVET

A NOVEL

HEATHER STROMMEN

PUBLISH **HER**™

VELVET © Copyright 2022 Heather Strommen

All rights reserved. No portion of this book may be reproduced, stored in a retrieval system, or transmitted in any form or by any means—electronic, mechanical, photocopy, recording, scanning, or other—except for brief quotations in critical reviews or articles, without the prior written permission of the publisher.

Company and/or product names may be logos, trade names, trademarks, and/or registered trademarks, and are the property of their respective owners.

This is a work of fiction. Names, characters, places and incidents are products of the author's imagination or are used fictitiously. Any resemblance to actual persons, living or dead, is entirely coincidental.

ISBN: 979-8-9850242-9-6 (Hardcover)
ISBN: 979-8-9865220-1-2 (Softcover)
Printed in the United States of America
First Printing: 2022

Published by Publish Her, LLC
2909 South Wayzata Boulevard
Minneapolis, MN 55405
www.publishherpress.com

Cover art by Noah Saterstrom
Cover design by Kayla Franz
Author photo by Belén Fleming

For Baba, my Ditty

"Show me your garden and I shall tell you what you are."

–Alfred Austin

PROLOGUE
WHAT IF?

I wonder what would have happened if my daddy had chosen to stay. What if he wrestled with sleep, kicking his legs one at a time out of the patchwork blanket Ditty had made for him and Mama, restless and unsettled and ready to run, even while Mama slept peacefully beside him, believing the man she loved and me, their sweet baby girl, were all nestled in, safe beneath the moon that hung above our home on Tender Vine Lane? What if, when his feet hit the floor, not really knowing why, instead of reaching for his wallet and watch, he took a big sip of water, swallowing the urge to leave? When Mama felt him stir, she reached for him, her skin touching his, the warmth of her love sending a shiver of guilt straight down his spine as he looked at his getaway outfit hanging over the corner chair—blue jeans and bowling alley jacket—and his cowboy boots next to the chair, all ready and waiting for him to run?

What if he made his way to the bathroom, caught a glimpse of himself in the mirror and asked himself why he wanted to go? He didn't talk about it or know how to explain it, and nobody would understand. Even his best friends at the bowling alley didn't know there was a darkness that had crept in and gotten a tangled hold on his thoughts. What if his reflection, the look in his eyes, the brokenness buried there was too much for him to bear, so he turned away, quickly avoiding his own gaze?

What if he kept walking, one foot in front of the other to my room, where a nightlight shaped like angel wings lit up my crib, the edges of my 6-month-old lips and my baby hair, twisty from the bath he and Mama had given me hours before? What if he paused next to me, felt the flesh of his own heart beating and started to cry silent tears that dripped one by one, like rain from the tips of the tree leaves after the storm ends and all that's left is the wind moving gently through?

What if, when he started to think everything was coming undone, he prayed to God to give him the courage and the desire to stay? The Bible says all you need is a mustard seed of faith, and the good Lord will take you home. What if he said a prayer for a tiny bit of courage, kissed my soft cheek, lingered in my freshly bathed smell, tousled my curls with his fingertips and walked back to his room to Mama? What if he slid into bed beside her quietly, and the heat of her back provided some comfort? What if he was relieved by his sudden decision to stay, even if his heart still felt unsettled? Even if his eyes darted back and forth between the moon and his boots like they were fighting and couldn't find rest.

CHAPTER ONE
STRIKE ZONE CHAMP

Mama has always said to ask whatever I want about my daddy, and now that I'm almost 16 I'm ready to know more. "Go ahead, Velvet," she says with a toughness about as strong as cardboard. "I ain't got nothing to hide when it comes to that man." Mama stands firm but her eyes portray a weakness, like a shot glass with a crack in it.

I have to admit, it's hard to make any sense at all of my daddy. Sometimes in quiet moments I want to ask Mama why he really left, or if he ever tried to come back. But something always stops my heart. I'm too afraid I'll end up hurting hers. Diamond Jim was the love of Mama's life. I know from the cries I hear deep in the night when her door is shut tight. Mama's tears remind me his leaving not only broke her heart, it also left a hole in mine.

I've never had a put-together mama like all the other kids in town do. Mine is different, and I am a little bit too because of it. My mama has a past, one she's proud of (so she says), and in Sack City everyone knows everyone's business (so she also says). And maybe she's right, because it's no secret Mama was involved with Diamond Jim, my daddy.

All the kids I know have parents who love each other, eat dinner together, go to church together—everything together. I know what everyone is saying, because I hear the whispers: "Who is Velvet's daddy? Why did he run off? I bet it's 'cause her mama is crazy. That's what happens to strippers."

I've heard all the rumors, and I let them spill off peoples' tongues and linger in the air because the truth is I have no idea what the real answers are. Sometimes Mama does do crazy things, but I think most of the time it's the alcohol talking. She doesn't mean to be ornery or bad; she's trying to protect the cracked shell covering the holes in her heart. I love how she protects with a fierceness, her own dignity, despite what living in a small town has done to break her down. People in Sack City don't like "different" too much. This I know for sure.

Mama says, "Oh, Velvet, your daddy was as handsome as they come. He was rugged, and he smelled like hard work and pine." She inhales deeply. "The way he smelled kept me coming back for more."

Sometimes I go to the dime store and open the tops of the aftershaves and smell the different scents, wondering—is this what hard work and pine smells like? I wonder which one was his favorite.

Mama doesn't know it, but sometimes I walk to the bowling alley after school to stare at Diamond Jim's picture, which hangs in the hallway on the way to the ladies' room. He's wearing an emerald green short-sleeved bowling shirt with a brown patch above his heart, his name in white script across it. His eyes have a special sparkle, and I pretend it's because he knows I'm staring straight at him and he's happy to see me. His hair is a deep brown, almost black, and parted on the side. His bangs stay put with some sort of gel, and I imagine they feel stiff and sticky. Below his picture a silver plate reads "Hall of Fame, Strike Zone Champ." My daddy was a bowling champion! I know it isn't much, but somehow that picture makes me feel proud.

I've had to attend birthday parties and get-togethers with friends at the bowling alley, and nobody my age really knows Diamond Jim is my daddy except for Mercy, but Mercy knows everything 'cause she's my best friend. The other kids run right past his picture without so much as a pause on their way to the pinball machines, but me, I get stuck. My feet feel anchored to the floor with no intention of moving in any direction. My friends tell me to hurry up or I'll be the last to play, but I don't care.

Through the years, Mama has given me bits and pieces of details, but sometimes I need to figure things out for myself. I'm sure he loved to bowl. I wonder if he still does. One time I stared so long and hard at his picture the manager of the alley came up and asked if I needed any help. I told him I was waiting on a friend, and he smiled and nodded, probably thinking, "That there is poor little Velvet, come to stare at her daddy again."

Every time I'm about to leave, I take one last look around to see if anyone's watching me, and when the coast is clear, I put my finger on his name tag and bless him. *Lord, wherever he is, please let him feel at this moment somebody loves him.* I step away slowly without breaking eye contact and wonder all the way home if he thinks of me or Mama.

CHAPTER TWO
MY NAME IS VELVET

The assignment was simple: Write about the meaning of your name. But its simplicity left me with an ache in my belly. I wish I had some magical story about why Mama chose my name. Like my best friend, Mercy, who is named after her great grandmother, Martha. Mercy keeps a framed black-and-white picture of her great grandmother on her dresser. It is rich in history and adds real significance to who Mercy is as a person.

In homeroom, the boy who sits next to me is named Danny. He's named after his daddy. He's always eating his pencils down to little nubs. The girl behind me, Elizabeth, is pretty and dresses well. She goes by Beth and has her mother's middle name. Beth's mom is the president of the volunteer organization at school, and Mama says she's a know-it-all who has her nose turned up in the air. Trudy, the quiet girl who sits in the front row, is named after her great aunt. Billy, a scrawny tall boy who always picks his nose, is named after his daddy. I've seen him wipe his boogers under his desk, and it makes me sick.

It seems like everyone in my school has a simple explanation for how they got their name. And by simple, I mean they wouldn't be embarrassed to get up in front of the class to explain it. I wish

I had a simple explanation for how I got mine. I've always had a yearning in my heart to have a sweet story like Mercy, Daniel, or even Elizabeth.

But I don't. Mama says she named me Velvet because I was conceived in the back of Diamond Jim's shiny black Cadillac, which happened to be smothered in a rich red velvet interior. And it's the honest-to-God truth!

Mama never seems to be embarrassed about it. She'll tell anybody who asks and always with a hint of pride in her voice. Like shacking up with a stranger outside the Hip Joint is something to be proud of.

"Oh, Velvet," she'll say, "that fabric was so luxurious. And the color red ignited passion and love."

I guess the saying "smooth like velvet" had to come from somewhere, and I can't help but think my mama coined the phrase.

Sometimes I feel bad about being born 'cause I think I remind Mama of the consequences of making bad decisions at the Hip Joint, even though it has been closed for many years and is currently the Suds 'n' Duds Laundromat. Father Matthew always says, "God makes all things new," and in this case God sure followed through.

As I've gotten older, I have to say the thought of the little encounter in the back of Diamond Jim's Cadillac kinda makes me cringe. I mean, who wants to imagine her mother having sex in the back seat of a car, no matter how nice the car may be? And with a man named Diamond Jim! Who even goes by such a name? Mama says his real name is David James, but she called him DJ for short. I wonder if he's named after somebody special, like his daddy, my granddad, or maybe even his grandfather, my great granddaddy.

Thankfully, my middle name is Mary, like our Lord's mother. I guess Mama threw it in to sanctify the deal. I know there was a rosary hanging from the rearview mirror of DJ's car, because Mama told me about how it swayed back and forth while he drove. Makes me feel good knowing our Lord and Savior was present on the night I was conceived. Personally, I think he blessed me right into this world.

I used to wish my name were Charlotte 'cause it sounds Southern and wholesome and sweet. Then maybe I'd live in a pretty white house with a big porch wrapped all the way around the front. I might skip in black patent shoes down perfectly groomed sidewalks in a pretty dress with flowers bursting off it. But I know better than to wish for such things. My life might not be as pretty or perfect as Charlotte's, but it's what God gave me.

So my name is Velvet, and I'm not proud of how I got my name, but it's the truth, and I am a fan of the truth. Lies get you in a heap of trouble, so when people ask me how I got such a unique name, I say my mama loved the feel of velvet. And boy, did she ever! Over the years, I've grown to love my name, even if I don't love the way I got it. It's unique to me. And in the end, it doesn't matter what other people think.

CHAPTER THREE
CONTEMPLATOR

When I was much younger, I overheard my Pops say to Ditty and Mama that I had a "contemplative heart." Actually, what I heard was, "You know, Velvet knows God in a real special way."

Ditty said, "What's it called again when someone thinks a lot about one thing that matters to them?"

"I think it's when you contemplate on something," said Mama. "Yes, that's what it is." Mama took a long drag of her cigarette. "She's a contemplator."

On my morning walk to school, I repeated the word over and over again so I wouldn't forget it. When I got there, I ran straight to Merriam-Webster's dictionary, propped the heavy book on my lap and started my search. I looked through the gold letters at the top of the pages, sounding it out—ca, can, co, con—as best as I could recall. Sadly, I couldn't find contemplator, but I did come across the word contemplative. I read the definition and knew it was the one! Basically, it said someone who is contemplative knows God and prays. I smiled as I closed the book, happy to learn I'm someone who knows God and even happier my family noticed.

Truth is, God and I do have a real special relationship. It started in Ditty and Pops' backyard, on a wooden swing hung under the wide oak tree. It was one of those summer nights when your belly is full, and you have dirt under your fingernails from playing. It was right before dusk. The light hit right, and everything looked alive. The air was warm, and the back and forth movement of the swing created a breeze against my skin. With every push forward, I'd reach my face toward the sky and feel it all.

My hair was longer then, brown with wavy curls that flew up into the air when I was up high and tickled my back on the way down. I remember it so clearly: My palms gripping the worn, dry rope while I hummed a tune Pops used to whistle. My eyes chasing the lightning bugs as I giggled in delight at the wonder of it all. It was there I heard God. I know it sounds crazy 'cause I was younger then, but when you hear God, you better believe you know who it is.

Isn't this beautiful, Velvet? The voice was so familiar, like I'd heard it thousands of times before.

"Yes!" I squealed, leaning into the air. "It's the most beautiful thing I've ever seen."

I made this all for you.

I continued swinging, smiling from ear to ear. "Thank you!"

That's how it went with God and me. And ever since then, I've had constant humming inside me, a tune I can't turn off. Wherever I am, there it is. When I'm sad, it brings me peace. When I'm scared, it surrounds me and holds me until I'm comforted. It's my song and it's God's song. It's our song together.

Somehow, in his own mighty way, he makes even heartache beautiful. And without him ... well, I wouldn't have the strength I need to live alongside Mama's pain.

I've needed God on many occasions, especially when I wondered about my daddy. Mama and I live in a trailer park on the north end of town. The entrance to the park has a white sign with camp green letters that read Simpler Times Cabins. I'm not sure why they call trailer homes cabins. Maybe because people think they're visiting and not really here to stay. On the other side of the street attached to wide wooden poles are five faded and worn solid-colored flags—red, yellow, blue, green and white fabric—that swoosh and sway in every passing breeze. On a windy night, when my window is open, the sound they make is the lullaby that sings me to sleep.

If you were passing through and saw those flags, you might think, wow! Something must really be going on here! Like some sort of amusement park or county fair. When I was young, I remember sitting in the front seat of Mama's pickup truck, windows down. I stuck my head out the window as we rounded the bend onto Tender Vine Lane and asked about the flags.

"Mama, what do those flags mean?"

She replied, "Not everything has to mean something, Velvet. They're hanging up on those damn poles and that's all."

I hate it when Mama swears. And maybe she's right. Some things are what they are.

I wish Mama felt the way I do about Sack City. She hates being in such a small town; she's always felt stuck. She tries to instill in me a wish for something more, something bigger. She says, "Velvet, you'd best make something out of yourself before this town and all its muck pull you under."

Ditty says, "Oh, Velvet, your mama is a big talker. She ain't ever leaving 'cause she thinks that old fool is gonna come back."

That old fool is my daddy.

Sack City is small. Mama says it's suffocating and full of hypocrites. She also says the women line up for church in their fancy dresses holding pretty pocketbooks and whispering ugly things that are none of their business about their neighbors. I try to tell her not everyone is like that, but she shakes her head and says, "You don't see what I see, Velvet."

The truth is, I don't.

I don't believe God gave me a contemplative heart for nothing, though. In fact, I think he gave me a forgiving way of understanding the world. Mama sees hypocrites; I see people trying their best. Mama sees women gossiping; I see them wishing they had just a little bit of her courage. Mama sees no way out and I see—even in Sack City—God can make a way. Even if it's staying right where you are.

I love walking down the street and knowing who lives in every home. I know Mrs. Johnson's cat, Mr. Jenkins, became her very best friend after her husband died, and every Sunday night she makes her late husband's favorite pot roast supper and sets an empty plate on the table for him. I know after dusk the baseball field lights up in all the right ways, making it the perfect place for teenagers to find each other's lips. And the bells at Our Savior's Bleeding Heart Church chime on the hour every hour, reminding us (well, me, anyway) that God is right here in Sack City.

Sometimes late at night, when the whole town is sleeping, I stare through my window at the moon. You ever have one of those nights where you know God wants to start a conversation? Well, it happens to me a lot. I don't realize it at first. Usually, I'm frustrated I can't fall asleep. I'll fuss and fidget in my bed, which is pushed up against the wall. Sometimes I get so restless I kick my feet up the wall and let my hair hang off the edge of the mattress. Then it hits me, a feeling God is waiting on me.

Father Matthew says, "God desires to be in a relationship with you, sort of like a best friend." Once after church, he explained his homily to me personally. "You wouldn't neglect your best friend, now, would you?"

If I ignored Mercy? She'd be madder than a hornet. But more important, it would hurt her heart. And I couldn't stand for that.

When I talk to God, I always look up or out a window, searching for him in places other than right where I am.

Mama usually leaves the porch light on at night—well, she has to really, 'cause Pops "fixed" it so good it stays on forever now—and it flickers across my sheets when the train rumbles by. I lie there and watch the light flash on and almost off. That's when the prayers pour out. Like a bucket full of water quenching the dry patches that ache for more and filling holes I didn't know were empty. Even though our porch light is a bit shaky, I'm happy there's any light at all.

CHAPTER FOUR
THE POWER VESTED IN ME

The picture of my daddy at the bowling alley is the only picture I've ever seen of him. Mama never told me it was there, I just happened upon it. One minute I was getting candy from the vending machine and the next my bowling shoes were stuck like chewing gum to the floor, my eyes fixed on his. Maybe God led me to it?

Mama says Diamond Jim left when I was 6 months old. He slipped out in the middle of the night without any rhyme or reason. "I woke up to an empty bed, a crying baby, and his dirty underwear still laying on the bathroom floor."

I bet if I could see into her heart, I would know more about why he left. There had to be signs along the way; maybe Mama wasn't paying any attention. I've heard that saying "it takes two to tango," and I think Mama and Diamond Jim must have been dancing to two different songs. But why?

I wonder if Diamond Jim tried to keep me safe the way cribs have rails that slide up to keep babies out of harm's way. The night he disappeared, did he gently pull down the rail and touch my cheek, his tears dropping on the yellow chenille blanket next to me? Did he pull it back up to lock it firmly in place before he left? Was he trying to protect me?

Truth is, I have no idea if my daddy even said goodbye to me. I imagine he drove away in the darkest part of the night, leaving me in my crib and Mama alone in a bed made for two. I wonder if he knows that the night he left he took Mama's spirit with him. There's a heavy feeling you get when you know you've hurt someone—a pit in your stomach that gnaws at you. You can try all you want and pretend it's not there, but you can't really hide from it. The second you slow down and get still, it grows and festers. You can stay busy enough to keep it at bay, but in those quiet moments when it's just you and your thoughts, you know. I wonder how my daddy handles those moments—when sleep won't come, and the sun doesn't rise for hours. I wonder if he feels it as he starts his day, brushing his teeth, eating his breakfast. I wonder if he feels something so unexplainable, so uncomfortable, that he never finds stillness. Maybe it's a whisper unexpectedly calling out her name. It starts gently, "Lynette ... Lynette ... Lynette ..." Or maybe it's "Velvet ... baby V ... my girl ..." and it gets louder and louder until he has to leave the house to find peace. Or maybe I'm silly, and he gets up every day and doesn't even think about Mama and me at all.

I've never been anywhere but Sack City. As quaint as it is, it seems to have a secret code of conduct everyone is in on except Mama. Ditty says the people of Sack City act like Jesus is the mayor. I can't help but laugh 'cause I think Jesus is too busy saving souls.

Sack City is a sidewalk-to-sidewalk town, unless you live in the trailer park like I do. We have cement curbs separating the street and the grass. I can always tell when I'm almost home 'cause Mercy and I start to walk on the edge of the curb, teetering between green grass and asphalt.

Most homes in town are different colors of brick. The ones on Ripple Street have front porches built for looking at the center of town and all its goings-on. Those are my favorites. Mama calls 'em rich folk houses. Every spring the cherry blossom trees bloom in front of those houses, filling the sidewalks with soft pinkish white petals that fall in pairs.

We're Catholic. At least that's the church we go to when Mama decides we need to go, which, truthfully, hasn't been for a while. Our church, Our Savior's Bleeding Heart, sits on one end of Main Street in town. It's red brick with two wood doors painted dark green. It's heavy, strong and rooted, like a tornado could pass through and tear everything up and it'd still be standing.

St. Stephen's Lutheran Church is on the opposite end of Main Street. It's a simple white clapboard box with a big white steeple on top and a pretty red door.

Both churches have bells, and every Sunday there's a bell ringing contest, or so Ditty says. One bell dings, and the other one dings louder. If it is a contest, I think the Catholics are winning 'cause they've got a bigger bell. So Sundays in Sack City are a clashing of big bells, but somehow, it's still beautiful despite all the dramatics.

The Main Street Diner and Sam's Hardware Store are nestled between the churches and other buildings on Main Street. The diner is a staple in town, with a big red awning over the front window and a neon open sign blinking on and off. Pops and I used to sneak away to the diner and share a grilled cheese with a salty buttered top and a big sweet pickle on the side.

The hardware store has wooden chairs out front that Sam himself made. In the summer, he sits out there greeting people as they pass by while his grandson Tommy runs the cash register inside.

Finally, there's a pie shop on Main Street called Bigsby's, which belongs to the infamous Mrs. Joan Evans. Mrs. Evans bakes homemade pies every morning, and all of Main Street smells like pie crust and jam.

Mama has a real dislike for Mrs. Evans—says she acts like she's the queen bee of Sack City. I once heard Mama say to Ditty, "There's not enough room in this town for her big mouth or her ass," and surprisingly Ditty shook her head in agreement.

One snowy winter night, Mama and I went to the diner for supper, which was a real treat for me. I don't remember how old I was, but I remember how I felt. We sat at the back of the diner in a cozy booth. Mama was wearing red high heels—she never cared about wearing the right shoes for the weather—and seemed genuinely happy. Until she didn't. I looked around to see what was making her so unsettled and saw Mrs. Evans and her family taking their seats at the big table toward the front of the diner.

Mrs. Evans was in a sensible jacket and stylish boots made for walking in slush and ice. With her were Mr. Evans—tall, dressed in a suit, his tie slightly loosened—and their daughter, Janet, who's my age and not very friendly. Mr. Evans got up to use the restroom while Mrs. Evans spoke to the waitress.

"We'll have the ..." And that's when I knew she saw us, or

rather she saw Mama seeing her. The waitress waited for Mrs. Evans to continue her order, but silence hung heavy in the air. Mama filled it by tapping the heel of her shoe against the baseboard of the booth. Click, click, click. Mrs. Evans shifted uncomfortably in her chair while Mama continued to tap her heel.

"Mama? Is something wrong?" I looked under the booth at her shoes. Mama smiled with her mouth closed, and I realized the problem with living in a small town. At any moment memories can come up, good or bad, and take a seat right beside you whether you want them to or not.

At the end of the Evans' table, the waitress shifted from foot to foot in her new white Keds. Mrs. Evans appeased the waitress, saying, "We'll all have the diner special, please."

Mama clicked her heel hard one last time, loud enough to make Mrs. Evans squirm.

I watched Mr. Evans return, rub Mrs. Evans' back and whisper, "It's fine," and I wanted to believe him. Mama placed her napkin on her lap like a lady with manners and began to eat.

I've never really known why Mama doesn't like Mrs. Evans. All I know is Mama is not impressed with her snoopy personality. "Velvet, don't ever make somebody try to like you. Either they do or they don't."

I guess Mrs. Evans doesn't like Mama too much either, but Mama doesn't seem to care whether people like her or not. She just doesn't.

In Sack City, the store owners know everyone's name. Most of them ask, "How's your mama, Velvet? You tell her we haven't seen her in a while."

I always tell Mama about the greetings, and she mumbles, "Huh. Seems like you can't make one itty-bitty move without the whole damn town wondering what you're doing."

Sorry for Mama's swearing, Lord.

"They were simply saying it'd be nice to see you is all."

"Yeah, yeah," she says.

Sack City is small enough I don't need a ride to school. Most days, Mercy and I walk together. But there are days when I have to go by myself, and those days I dread the most. With Mercy, it doesn't matter what I'm wearing or who my daddy is. On the days without Mercy, I do everything I can to hold my head high, but I can feel the stares and hear the whispers.

It's no secret my daddy ran off and left Mama. Mama was a dancer at the Hip Joint before it was destroyed by a mysterious fire. She says the Hip Joint was her happy place, and she'll never forgive Mrs. Evans and the hypocritical city council for having it burned to the ground. Of course, these are just rumors, but I listen to Mama like they're real 'cause sometimes she needs to be heard.

I can tell by the way she talks about dancing that on stage was where Mama came to life. "Velvet, up there under those dim lights, I was somebody else. My body moved beat by beat and I built my confidence. There wasn't one damn woman in this whole town who didn't wish she could do what I was doing."

The owner of the Hip Joint decided rebuilding from scratch would be too much work. There were openings for dancers in nearby towns, but Mama said those establishments were too seedy and showed too much skin. So she retired from dancing—

though she often still wears her dancing boots—and had to get a real job, which she believes robbed her of her creative spirit.

Now Mama works as a receptionist at Sullivan's Auto Body, and I often stop in after school to say hi. The owner, Mr. Mikey Sullivan, is her old high school sweetheart. He flirts with Mama, and I can tell he still likes her by the way he smiles at her, but Mama says he doesn't light a fire in her like Diamond Jim used to.

Because the Hip Joint once stood across the street from where Sullivan's Auto Body is, I imagine Mama spends most of her time staring out the window reminiscing about days long past. I can tell she's bored. She twiddles her thumbs and swivels her chair from side to side. The shoes she used to dance in, now get caught in the nubby carpet beneath her desk. I know she'd rather be practicing a dance routine or gluing rhinestones onto a skirt for a new show costume. But instead, she seems stuck to that metal chair, heavy and hopeless like her pockets are filled with lead weights.

We don't have much money to spare, so sometimes I wear bits and pieces of Mama's old dancing costumes—pared down a bit, of course. Ditty likes to sew, thank goodness, and she adds to my wardrobe by making me a wide array of skirts and tops that look similar to what other girls are wearing. I always have something of Mama's on, though, like a jacket or a scarf.

Janet Evans sticks to the style her mother has bestowed upon her, and I do admire the clean and perky way she dresses, with her tweed skirts and pretty buttoned sweaters and mahogany penny loafers that click and clop around the halls of the school.

As a freshman, she's the queen of style, and the boys seem to flock to her honey and get caught up in her sticky sweet hum.

My appreciation for Janet's fashion doesn't hide my concern for the state of her heart, though. Janet is always one to comment on my wardrobe. One day at school, she said, "Oh, Velvet, did your Mama loan you her sweater?"

I looked down at my sequined patterned sweater and suddenly felt not good enough. Janet looked at her best friend, Sandra Shaw, and they smirked at each other like they were saying something without actually saying it. They were wearing matching crisp white shirts with navy blue sweaters resting around their shoulders.

Mercy was quick to jump in, "Velvet, I've never seen that pretty sweater before."

And I loved her even more.

When I told Mama how Janet and Sandra behaved, she said, "They're jealous," and then she went into a rant. "Goddammit, this town is full of mean, uninspired, ugly women."

When Mama finally calmed down, she said, "Now, don't go gettin' your undies in a bundle over this, Velvet. It's not worth it. If any girl eyes you up and down and whispers to the girl next to her, you can bet your sweet ass jealousy is running like a wild hog straight to her brain. Once it's there, that hog will kick and snort and make a fuss because it knows it will never have the kind of style you have."

Mama has a way with words and making them feel like truth. After her speech, I couldn't help but picture Janet and Sandra making the sounds of wild pigs.

Mama still had her dancing career when I was in elementary

school, and lots of men were interested in her then. I know this 'cause Mama made sure to let me know. "Men were lined up and around the corner to see your mama dance," she'd say when she came home still in costume. I always thought she was so glamorous—hair done up high on her head, fancy shoes clicking on the linoleum. She'd kiss me goodnight before she showered, and she always smelled like hairspray and beer. The dancing kept her busy, I'm sure of this, 'cause she was out late most nights, and Ditty and Pops spent the evenings with me.

I never really noticed how our family was so different until the night of my fourth grade Bring Your Parents to School event. When I made the invitation, instead of writing "Dear parents," I had to write "Dear parent." At the event, I saw other kids arm in arm with both of their parents and had to blink back the tears pushing at my eyes.

Mama noticed I was upset and whispered in my ear, "Velvet, now you look at me." When I obeyed, she said, "I don't need no man to help me raise my child." I nodded like I agreed. "God only gives you what you can handle, and by the power vested in me, I've been handling it fine."

Mama grabbed my hand, and we pushed past all the parents to the welcome table.

Now, I had never been to an actual wedding, but I had seen enough on TV to know better. "Mama," I said, "by the power vested in me is what a pastor says to announce the bride and groom are husband and wife."

Mama giggled and pulled me in tight. "Oh, it doesn't matter how you use it, as long as you say it with conviction."

"Welcome to parents' night," Mrs. Evans said as she checked people in.

I saw what she did with her mouth when she noticed Mama. It was the same smile Janet used on me.

"Lynette, is that you? My goodness, we haven't seen you around the school in quite some time."

She looked Mama up and down, taking in Mama's long magenta coat tied in front, which hid her dancing costume perfectly. No one knew Mama was a "nurse" underneath her coat, with a garter belt hugging her thigh. Without making eye contact, Mama let out a faint "uh-huh" in response to Mrs. Evans, as if actually speaking to her would draw out the already uncomfortable interaction.

"Is it just you then, Lynette?" Mrs. Evans cleared her throat and whispered, "Or will Velvet's daddy be attending?"

Mama planted her boots firmly on the floor, lifted her chest high, and balled up her fists. I grabbed hold of one of 'em, quick and tight.

"Mama, I've been dying to show you my art project," I said. "Let's go this way."

I steered her out of trouble and toward my painting of a fern, but it didn't stop her from looking back at Mrs. Evans, who looked up from checking in the next family and gave Mama a small wave.

It's clear to me now that even back then, Mama had a way of being broken but still strong, like a bird that falls from a tree. She wasn't ready to spring for the sky and fly again, but she wasn't about to lie there and die, either. Thankfully, Mama still has a spunky, sassy, confident side. A side that says don't even think about messing with Lynette Underwood!

CHAPTER FIVE
THE BLUE JOURNAL

L ast night I had one of those restless, kicking my feet up the wall kind of nights. I tried talking to God and even got real, real quiet, but I didn't hear anything back. I walked to the bathroom, noticed Mama's bedroom light on and tiptoed in. Mama had fallen asleep reading a magazine article, "20 Ways to Be a Better Mother." I set the magazine on the bedside table next to her cigarettes and was about to turn off her light when I noticed a blue journal lying beside her and a pen wedged in between its pages.

I felt an urge to open it and read what Mama wrote but stepped away instead. What did I want to know? I went back to my room, still restless and unable to fall asleep. I tossed and turned, my eyes jumping from wall to the window. I couldn't stop thinking about that blue journal and the pen that knew her secrets.

It's Sunday afternoon and Mama is asleep again, but she's propped upright on the living room sofa this time. The TV is on, and I can faintly make out sounds of a soap opera. The couple in it is promising nothing will ever break them apart. Ditty has gone to the grocery store, and I'm coming out of the shower. I glance into Mama's room to see if the journal is sitting on her nightstand. I inch toward it like it's calling my name, but slowly, like I'm scared of it. My heart pounds as I pick it up, open to the page where the pen is and read:

Does he think he can get away with being a coward? 'Cause that's what he is! And what makes him think he's so special anyway? He wanted something and got to act on it without any thought or care. He has a baby girl who needed him—who still needs him, goddammit! But he's nowhere to be found. I hope guilt follows him around like a mad coyote in broad daylight. I hope it festers, like my pain, circling around his life, making living hard to do.

My stomach tightens. I push the hurt away from my eyes. She's talking about him—my daddy. I continue reading as my free hand clutches her white bedspread, making it bunch beneath my fingers. I take a deep breath and continue:

He thinks he can up and leave? And for what? Another woman? A better one? I was his woman. He had a good one, a great one—he was just too blind to see it. He had the best already, he'll never find another one like me, that ragged-ass coward of a man.

My heart aches for Mama. I get up and poke my head around the door frame to see if she's still sleeping. The coast is clear. I scan the front of the journal and see Mama's writing along the binding:

Lord, I miss him. Will he come back? Please say he'll be back. I pray you will quiet this pain.

I wipe away a tear. Who is this other woman? Why wasn't Mama enough? How long ago did she write these words? Does she still feel this way now? Is this still her prayer? I hear the front door open as Ditty walks in with the groceries. I place the journal back on the nightstand just the way I found it and exit Mama's room. I head straight to the bathroom and run the faucet for a few moments. I talk to God like he's sitting on the toilet the way Mercy sits there when I'm running late for school: *I knew she struggled, Lord. But I didn't know how much. Her words gave me a glimpse into her heart, and now I need to know more. I have to know the truth. Why am I so afraid?*

I exit the bathroom and whistle nervously. Without offering Ditty any help with the groceries, I walk into my bedroom. Nothing looks the same. My bed, the window—it all feels different. I feel different.

Now that Ditty's here, I won't be able to sneak back into Mama's room. I'll have to wait. There are so many pages, so many words. My heart is heavy with this new knowledge.

Guilt starts to creep in. How could I violate Mama like this? I'm ashamed of how easily I get frustrated with her for not living like other mothers do, like Mercy's mom or even Mrs. Evans.

Ditty's unpacking of the groceries stirs Mama from her nap and up off the couch. She walks past my bedroom into hers, and I see her in a new way. I hear the sound of her door shutting and catch my breath.

In school, we're reading "To Kill a Mockingbird," and I keep thinking Mama and Atticus Finch have similar personalities. The whole town is against them, even though they're trying to do the right thing with the tools they've been given. The people of Sack City seem to have an opinion about how Mama is experiencing life without truly knowing her experience. Atticus says, "You never really know a man until you stand in his shoes."

In Mama's case, you never really know a woman until you've danced in her boots. Or read her journal.

At school the next day, I'm consumed with thoughts of Mama's journal. During English class, my teacher, Mrs. Holden, says, "Velvet, tell us why the author, Harper Lee, chose Scout to be the narrator."

I'm so lost in my thoughts I don't even hear the question.

"Velvet?"

"I'm sorry, ma'am. Can you repeat the question please?"

All eyes are on me, but I don't care. Mama's world is inside that journal, and I need to go back inside and figure out what happened.

Mrs. Holden gives me a look of disapproval, something I'm not used to, and asks Janet Evans instead. Janet straightens her shoulders and sits up taller. "He chose Scout because she was the youngest and she could tell the story through childlike eyes."

I have to agree with Janet. Only Scout could tell Atticus' story, 'cause she had ... what's it called ... compassion!

Suddenly, I feel like Scout, who wanted her town not to punish her daddy and who was trying to save an innocent man. If I knew more, I could help Mama find Diamond Jim and heal her heart. Maybe then everyone in Sack City will finally leave Mama alone.

I know if I go straight home from school I can read more. I haven't told Mercy yet about what I found, and for some reason I don't want to share it. I'm not ready. But Mercy wants to go to Bigsby's and is charmingly relentless.

"Velvet, don't you wanna get pie today? All I've been thinking about is warm apple pie."

"I told Mama I'd get supper going before she gets home." I lie like it's easy to do. *Lord, forgive me.*

Mercy looks at me and raises one eyebrow. "Did you, now?" She knows I'm up to something 'cause she knows me too well.

"We can go get pie and a cream soda tomorrow," I say, nudging her with my shoulder.

She smiles. "Promise?"

I put my pinky finger up for her to hook hers onto. "Promise," I say and walk toward Tender Vine Lane at a pace Mercy isn't used to.

"What kind of supper are you making anyway? Why we gotta move so quick?"

"I want to get the table ready, you know, do something nice for Mama."

Each extra syllable is shaving precious time off my speed.

We reach the big tree where we always part, and I run off. "See you in the morning."

I look back and see Mercy watching me run. I sprint down the driveway. I swing open the front door ready to rush to Mama's journal when I hit a brick wall—or at least what feels like one.

"Why are you in such a hurry, Velvet?" Mama asks, wine in hand, standing in the middle of the living room. She's like a prize fighter defending her championship and blocking my way to the truth.

CHAPTER SIX
DIAMOND JIM

Mama has always loved her wine, but she didn't start drinking every day until I was about 10 years old. The Hip Joint had burned down, and Pops had recently passed. It started with one glass of wine with dinner and over the years moved to a whole bottle every night. I was too young to know it at the time, but with each sip of wine, Mama's spirit was shrinking. I guess having the Hip Joint and her own daddy around gave her what she needed to survive without Diamond Jim. Once both were gone, drinking became the most important part of her life. I guess me and Ditty aren't enough.

It's Thursday night. Ditty is going to bingo, and if Mama has enough drinks she'll pass out on the couch before dusk. I've never liked Mama's drinking. As a matter of fact, I hate it. But tonight, I keep wishing she'll have one more sip and another right after.

Like clockwork, her eyelids start to droop and she's out. I whisper her name. "Mama? Mama, are you up?" Nothing. I pick up her wine glass and set it down with a thud. Still nothing. Then I tiptoe to her bedroom, and before I enter, I turn back to check on her one more time. Still asleep! I have some time before she wakes up. I pick up the journal and read from the beginning:

I've got to get this all down. Every little detail, so I will never forget. I met someone tonight. Someone different. In a good way, I hope. At the end of my set, I tipped my sailor hat toward the front row and let my hair fall around my shoulders. That's when I saw him. He smiled at me like he knew me. His eyes held my gaze in the spotlight while the crowd clapped. I felt a rush of heat from within, and all I saw was him. Rodney turned off the spotlight, and our gaze broke. I turned my back and instantly felt an emptiness as I strutted in my red high heels back to the dressing room.

The other girls cheered and clapped as I entered the room. One of them said, "Damn, Lynette. You done left the crowd speechless." I asked if they saw the handsome man in the front row. Jenny stepped away from her dressing table and turned toward me. "Honey, that there is Diamond Jim, and you don't want any part of him." She shook her pointer finger near my face. "He's a notorious ladies' man." I didn't ask Jenny how she knows these rumors, and frankly I don't care.

Back inside the club, my eyes searched the room like a bobcat on the prowl. There he was, standing at the bar, staring at the door I'd come out of. I had to play it cool, so I pretended to be leaving. I flung my bag over my shoulder and took my own sweet time heading for the door.

"Can I buy you a drink, miss?" he asked. His voice was deep and inviting. I felt my body relax in a way it hadn't in a long time. I turned around and introduced myself.

"Miss Lynette Underwood, you sure were the prettiest dancer on stage tonight," he replied, touching my shoulder. My heart about burst out of my chest. All of a sudden, the room felt electric and alive. I tried desperately to hide my grin and reminded myself to play it cool. I said a drink would be nice.

He slipped a strong hand behind my back and touched me with a pressure that let me know he was there and a gentleness that left me wanting more. Two draft beers appeared at the bar, and I lit a cigarette. I was nervous. I asked his name, blowing smoke into the already smoky air.

"Oh my word, where are my manners?" he said as he wiped the condensation from his beer on his jeans and reached out his hand. "David James. Everyone calls me Diamond Jim. But you can call me DJ."

I took his hand and repeated his name. I prayed he wouldn't let go. I asked how someone gets a name like Diamond Jim.

He said, "I guess I was lucky a few times in the bowling hall, and my friends said everything I touched turned to diamonds. Somehow it just stuck."

Then he let my hand go and pulled his stool closer, so

our knees were touching. He was so close I could smell his aftershave—it was like hard work and pine.

I inhale the bedroom air like I can smell Diamond Jim, too. Like he's right here. I peek into the living room to see if Mama has moved. She's still out. I keep reading:

We ended up sitting and talking for two hours while Rodney cleaned and closed the bar. Rodney looked over at me a few times to make sure I was all right. I was more than all right. Men like Diamond Jim don't often show up in Sack City. Mikey Sullivan is just high school love, predictable and safe. DJ is a shot of pure adrenaline, quick and impulsive. I've never felt like this.

When Rodney turned off the neon sign, DJ took my hands and asked, "Can I give you a ride home, Lynette?" I watched my name roll off his lips like he'd said it thousands of times before.

DJ's shiny black Cadillac sat at an angle near the back of the parking lot. He opened the passenger door and touched my back as I slid into the car. To my surprise, the seats were covered in a red velvet, and it was soft and smooth against my legs. He shut the door, and I watched in the passenger side mirror as he walked around the car. He was confident and strong. He settled into his seat and put in a tape, and Elvis Presley's voice filled the air, low and persuasive. I swirled my fingertips around the velvet seats. A black rosary hung from the rearview mirror. Warm summer air blew through the windows, mixing with his pine cologne. I wasn't drunk, I'd only had one beer. But my head spun with delight. We drove out of the Hip Joint parking lot, not knowing where to go. The moonlight created a warm glow against the rich red velvet interior, and the rosary swayed from side to side, never losing momentum. DJ patted his hand on the seat, encouraging me to slide closer to him. I hesitated for a second and wondered if it was a good idea. I thought about Eve in the garden of good and evil. She must have sensed it wasn't a good idea to eat the forbidden fruit, but something made her do it. The plush fabric beneath my legs lit a fire of passion in me, and I knew I'd give in like Eve.

Oh, Mama. I close the journal hard. I have so many feelings. I feel overwhelmed and guilty. Mama is still taking her wine nap, but I don't want to risk getting caught. I look out the window toward the sky. *Lord, am I the consequence that comes from Mama's bad decisions?*

CHAPTER SEVEN

BINGO

I love a lot of things: the Lord; the smell of Ditty's cooking; summer nights sitting under the willow tree; Mama dancing in the living room when Elvis Presley sings; my memories of Pops; the quiet in the morning before Sack City comes to life; hanging out with Mercy; and going to play bingo at the VFW with Ditty.

Lucky for me, bingo happens every Thursday evening except Holy Thursday, and Ditty never misses it. When Pops was alive, he'd sometimes go, too. Those were my favorite nights 'cause he wasn't good at playing a lot of cards at once, and he needed my help. Ditty can manage about 15 cards on her own, but she brings me anyway, for luck.

"Velvet, I'm gonna need my good luck charm," she says pointing at my nose, "and that's you, little lady."

She pulls me in real tight, rubbing my luck against her as hard as she can, and I love the feeling.

I really hate to miss bingo, but it's been a week since I found the journal, and it's all I can do not to think about what else is written on those pages. If I can get Mama to go to bingo instead of me, I can read a little bit more. The moment she walks in from work I say, "Mama, I have a funny feeling tonight you're gonna win at bingo."

She frowns at me from the front door. "Really? Well, that'd be nice." She lights a cigarette and starts rambling on about her day.

"We had two crashed-up cars come in the shop and I've been doing paperwork all day. Would you believe Mr. Baxter drove his truck right off the road and hit old Mr. Miller's tractor parked in the field?"

Mama walks to the fridge with the cigarette hanging off her lips and pulls out a plate of thawed pork chops. "I mean, how does that happen? I think he fell asleep at the wheel."

I look up at the clock above the stove. It's 5:15 and Ditty will be over soon. She drives past Tender Vine Lane on her way to bingo, so she almost always comes to our house early and makes pork chops and applesauce. I'm so focused on getting Mama out of the house I don't even ask if Mr. Baxter is OK.

"Mama, when's the last time you went to bingo?"

Mama stops in the middle of the kitchen to think. "Hmm, I honestly cannot remember."

She opens an upper cabinet and reaches for a bottle of wine.

"I think it's time! Besides, you need to do something for fun!"

Mama pauses and looks at me. "It's kind of you to think of me having fun and all, but I want to sit at home and unwind. Sitting in a smoky hall with a bunch of old mothers of women I don't talk to sounds awful. No, thank you!"

Mama reaches for her glass, clearly on a mission to get to her unwinding.

I hear Ditty pull into the gravel driveway. Before she even fully enters the house, she starts in on her plans for tonight's game.

"Sweetie, let's only bring the blue dotters," she says to me. "Because last week Louise used only purple dotters and it brought her luck. I like the idea of using one color for a change. You know, mix it up a little."

Most Thursdays, Ditty switches out the colors of her dotters from one round to the next. She starts with pink, moves on to blue, then green, and ends the night with purple—her favorite color.

"Ditty, I think Mama wants to go tonight."

Mama looks at me, and I look at Ditty, avoiding Mama's eyes.

"Velvet, did I not say I had no interest in going to bingo?"

Ditty chimes in, "You know, Lynette, I can't remember the last time you came to bingo. It might be good for you to do something different, something fun for a change."

Mama gives me the evil eye while I continue to look at Ditty for support. Anyway, Mama knows we're right. She turns on her heel, throws her hands in the air and says, "Well, for Chrissakes, I guess I'm going to bingo tonight."

I instantly say a silent prayer: *Lord, forgive her for bringing you into this bingo conversation. Especially since I'm the one pushing her to go.*

Ditty does a happy dance in front of the stove, turns the skillet on high and adds the oil. Mama's willingness to go is so sudden I haven't had time to figure out an excuse for not going. As Ditty adds the pork chops to the pan and Mama helps with supper, I pull out my notebook with a sigh and try my best to look overwhelmed.

"Velvet, what is all that grumbling?" Mama asks. "You never get worked up over your assignments. What's got your tail tied in a knot?"

"I forgot to finish my English paper." I pause, trying to think of the next thing to say. "I ... I need to do the bibliography." I think they believe me. "As much as I'd like to and all, I don't think I'll be going tonight."

I look up at Ditty. *Lord, forgive me right here and now for lying to Mama and Ditty, but I've got to read the journal!*

Ditty turns away from the stove and says, "All my friends have been asking if you'd sit nearby tonight, so some of your luck rubs off on them."

I feel my face flush. "That's so nice. Tell them next time I'll bring extra luck!"

After we eat, I tell Mama I'll clean up the dinner dishes. I hope she doesn't pick up on my eagerness for her to go. As the two of them get ready to leave, Ditty rubs my nose, pats my head and makes me kiss her lucky mini statue of the Virgin Mary before she walks out the door.

"You two have fun!" I say. "I hope you win!"

This, at least, is true.

They hop in Ditty's old blue sedan and drive off. When I no longer hear the crunching of gravel, I run to Mama's room. Her lights are off, so I make my way to the nightstand and flip on the table lamp. Is this what criminals feel like before they steal? I open the top drawer, and there's the journal. I find the page where I left off:

I think we were on a mission to follow the light of the moon 'cause wherever we were it was right there, too, lighting the narrow country roads. The corn stalks lining the sides of the road swayed gently as we passed. Elvis kept crooning, and I put my hand on DJ's leg. He sped up and my stomach leaped. He pulled over and turned off the engine and Elvis went silent. But I was still humming. When DJ leaned in for a kiss, the whole world stopped. I've never been kissed like that before.

Mikey Sullivan is good at a lot of things, and his kissing isn't bad, but it's like he hasn't quite figured out how to use his tongue. It certainly never leads to anything more than heavy petting and chapped lips. Mikey told me he wanted us to be each other's first, but something kept telling me to wait. Tonight, I know why.

DJ's kisses are tender and sensual. He uses his tongue like a man. He held my face in his hands, never missing a beat, and paused to look at me. Our lips parted for a moment, and I ached for them to return. My body wanted him, and he knew it. He slowly unbuttoned my blouse, kissing my neck and then my chest. I took it all in—the soft velvet fabric against my bare back, the warm night air swirling around us, the moon shining sweetly on his face—and I knew I was his.

As his hands made their way toward my skirt, Ditty's voice popped into my head, telling me to wait to have sex until I'm married: "You gotta save your pocketbook for a man who's ready to invest." I tried to push her voice away. I told myself DJ would be my husband. I tried to

*ask him to wait but struggled to get the words out. Then
I admitted I'd never done it before. I couldn't look him
in the eye. I was embarrassed 'cause I could tell he's
way more experienced than Mikey or me. DJ moves
like a professional race car driver who knows when to
turn, when to speed up, and when to slow down. With me
being a dancer and all, people assume I've been doing
the dance with no pants for a long time, but I haven't. I
always liked the idea of saving myself for my husband.
But tonight, DJ's engine was already revved up and ready
to go, and he put my body in full throttle. There was no
shifting those gears back to neutral.*

*He whispered in my ear, "You don't need to worry
about a thing, Lynette, I always get it right."*

*Then we made love. The sweetest love that's ever
been made. Right there in his Cadillac with its interior
smothered in red velvet, we became one. And after we
were done, we lay there together, no longer strangers.*

I can hardly believe my eyes. All these years, Mama has
been telling me the whole truth! I was conceived in the back
of a Cadillac, on top of red velvet interior, under the light of
the moon. But why didn't she wait? *Lord, forgive her. She knew
better. She did!*

I turn the page to the next entry:

*Tonight, Diamond Jim showed up early at the Hip Joint
and sent the girls into a tizzy. They ran into the dressing
room and told me he was sitting at the bar. One of the*

girls said, "Lynette, guess who's out there waiting for you?" I felt my face turn hot and Jenny chimed in, "Lynette, I told you he was trouble. I can tell by the way you're blushing you're about to dance for just one man out there tonight."

I know Jenny means well, I do, but she doesn't know the connection DJ and I have. It's not what she thinks it is. I am different for him. I can feel it.

Before my set, I slid up beside him at the bar and asked if I could buy him a drink. At the sound of my voice, he swiveled in his seat, put his hand on my lower back and replied, "Yes, ma'am, you can."

I wanted him to kiss me right then and there. We stared at each other for a few seconds without ordering or saying anything until Rodney announced I was on in five minutes.

"Break a leg, beautiful," DJ said, smiling that smile of his.

As I turned to leave, he kissed my neck, and my legs went weak. Pulling away from him was like torture. I headed toward the stage door and took a deep breath. One more dance and I was his. All his.

The music fired up for my signature sultry tap dance routine with high kicks and low lunges. As I took the stage, I looked out at the bar and spotted Joan Evans, with her long legs and fiery red hair, standing next to DJ. Either she already knew him or was trying to get to know him. She was laughing and smiling and tossing her hair back and forth. It looked like DJ was being friendly—

maybe. I made eye contact with him, and his face lit up like a kid entering the county fair on opening night. Joan Evans and her ginger mane had nothing on me. I was his. His eyes told me so.

When my routine came to its climactic end, I landed my final tap with power and poise. Rodney shined the spotlight directly on my face. Everyone in the room was staring me. The second the light went off, I hurried to the bar and stepped between DJ and Joan Evans. She must have thought she was settling in for the night with my man. But he leaned into me and whispered, "Do you want to go for a drive?" I grabbed his hand, and we walked right out the door with Joan Evans and the whole joint watching our every move.

DJ couldn't get the Cadillac unlocked fast enough. He slid into his seat and before he could even start the car, I straddled him, letting him know the only gears he needed to shift were mine. Let that be a lesson for Little Miss Ginger!

Mama! I guess this explains the friction between her and Mrs. Evans. Maybe Mrs. Evans loved Diamond Jim too.

I love Mrs. Evans' baked goods, but I very much dislike the way she treats Mama. It's like she's trying to be as sugary and sweet as her pie, but she's as fake as the wedges displayed under the glass dome next to the register. She always starts in with something courteous—like she should, owning a pie shop and all—but anything beyond hello is usually suspicious. She'll say, "Oh, hello, Velvet. What can I get for you today?" And then,

"Did your mama give you enough money for pie and a drink? You know it's not Monday, right?"

On Mondays, you get a glass of milk for free with every slice of pie. Truth is, I do try to go in on Mondays 'cause I don't usually have enough for a drink. And Mercy and I almost always share a piece of blueberry pie.

Mercy knows Mrs. Evans isn't kind about Mama. She has heard her say things like, "Velvet, I can't even imagine how your mama gets along without any help from a husband." I never know what to say back, so I don't say anything at all. Mercy says Mrs. Evans' tongue can't help but move when it shouldn't.

I realize Mama and Ditty will be back soon. Unless Ditty talks too long, which she loves to do. But I bet Mama will hurry her up so she can get home and drink her wine. Before I close the journal, I flip quickly through the pages, and my eye catches on four words:

Lynette Lucille, YOU'RE PREGNANT!

This is it! This is where I come into the story! As I pull the journal toward my chest, I hear car wheels on gravel. I panic. How did time go by so quickly? Mama will be inside in seconds. I shove the journal in the drawer with no time to worry about whether it's set in the right position. I hurry back to my homework, which is really just a blank sheet of paper. I take big, deep breaths to calm my heart.

I hear Mama laughing, and Ditty says, "Tell Velvet she's coming next time!"

Then Mama opens the door and says, "Velvet, you ain't gonna

believe this! I won $40 tonight! And guess who was sitting right across from me when I jumped up and shouted bingo?"

"Who?"

"Joan 'Ginger' Evans."

My body freezes.

"You shoulda seen the look on her face. Priceless, I tell you. I think I'm gonna start going to bingo more often, 'cause it sure felt good to win."

Mama looks at the unwashed dishes in the sink. "Velvet, how come these dishes aren't washed? You said you were taking care of them."

"I'll get right to it. I got tired after I finished my paper."

Lies. Is this who I am now?

Mama heads down the hall to her bedroom as I fill the sink with hot, soapy water. The steam fogs up the kitchen window, but I can still make out a blurred image of Mrs. Johnson's cat, Mr. Jenkins, who's waiting patiently outside her door.

Mama shouts, "Velvet, were you looking for something in my room?"

I inhale sharply—I left her light on.

"Ummm, yes," I shout back. "I was looking for a ..." Think, Velvet, think! "A nail file! I got a stupid hangnail and needed a nail file!"

I can tell by her footsteps she isn't too concerned. I imagine she's changing into her nightgown and putting her hair in curlers. I turn off the water. Before I dry my hands, I draw a heart around Mr. Jenkins in the condensation on the window.

Before I go to bed, I pray: *Lord, please forgive me. If I really shouldn't be reading Mama's journal, show me a sign. Maybe finding it is the sign? Maybe You want me to know so I can track down my daddy and tell him how much Mama loves him. How happy she'd be if he came back! I'll be listening for your answer. I love you. Amen.*

CHAPTER EIGHT
MERCY

I remember the day Mercy and I became best friends. My fourth grade teacher, Mrs. June, held onto Mercy's maroon cardigan-covered shoulders and said, "Class, we have a new student, and her name is Mercy Blessing."

The sound of her name rolling off Mrs. June's lips sounded like a sweet spring song. I looked up from my desk and saw Mercy and instantly loved everything about her, especially her name. Thankfully, Mrs. June sat Mercy right beside me, and as she settled into her seat, she spoke to me in a whisper: "Hi, I'm Mercy."

I whispered back, "Hi, I'm Velvet."

And instantly we were best friends.

Before I met her, I'd heard the word mercy on a few different occasions. Like when Ditty hears something troubling, it's "Lawd, have mercy." Or Mama might say, "Mercy, mercy me," shaking her head from side to side. Father Matthew and the congregation all say in unison, "Lord, have mercy," after the community prayers. So I've gathered over the years that mercy is what you say when things aren't going right or when someone is down on their luck. I've also gathered mercy is something you beg for when you need the Lord right quick.

My Mercy is a beautiful friend. She's the only friend I have ever truly confided in. She knows all my secrets, even the embarrassing ones, and the ones that are just dreams dancing around my heart. Mercy knows that I have a big crush on Bobby Johnson, my neighbor's grandson—even though Mama has no idea—and that I dream of kissing him at dusk, behind the baseball dugout, where the older teenagers go. He usually comes to his grandma's for supper on the weekends, and if I sit at the right angle in my kitchen chair, my neck stretched real long, I can see him eating his dinner. He's handsome, with short dark brown hair, and when he smiles, his dimples get real big.

Mercy is also the only person who knows about Mama's drinking. When I say to her, "Mama fell asleep again on the couch last night," she knows instantly what it means.

Once she said, "Velvet, maybe you should hide the wine, or pour it down the sink." Her eyes lit up like it was the best idea.

"She likes it too much," I said. "She'll get another bottle."

I've seen Mama, dog-tired, get up and go to the store, saying she's gonna get me a special treat. I know full well it's because her wine is running low. She comes back with a brown paper bag for herself and throws me a box of Cracker Jack like I've been begging for it all day. "Here you go, sweetie!"

Mercy knows my heart more than anyone else does. She's the only one who knows about the time God found me on the swing. She says, "Tell me the story again, Velvet, 'cause it gives me the holiest of goose bumps."

Mercy goes to the Lutheran church where the pastors can

be married. Mama doesn't think it's right to make the Catholic priests suffer like they do. "Poor Father Matthew," she says. "All alone in that big sanctuary."

Ditty always reminds Mama, "He chose that life for himself, so you don't need to be saying 'Poor Father Matthew.' He's living out a calling in his heart, Lynette."

Secretly, I think Mama has a crush on Father Matthew, 'cause he's the only man I've ever seen her put on extra makeup for. I wonder if it's the same way she put on makeup for my daddy, slow and deliberate, like each stroke of the brush is leading her closer to her destiny. Father Matthew has a way of making Mama smile real big and beautiful. I love seeing her with her cheeks all lit up pink like that 'cause I don't get to see her that way at home. You'd think with all the joy church gives her, she'd want to go to more often, but she doesn't

Mama says, "God is everywhere, Velvet. I don't need to sit in those pews to find him."

Mercy's parents met in high school and married as soon as they graduated. Mama loves Mercy, but I think she's a bit envious of her family. I've heard her say after a bottle of wine, "If I had a reliable partner like Mercy's daddy, I wouldn't be in this situation."

She likes to point out the "perfects" in other people's lives— happily married, clean house, homemade suppers, family prayers, and on and on. Mama forgets not everyone has a perfect life. I call these outbursts, PLMs, or Mama's "poor little me" moments.

Sometimes I tell Mama, "It's not Mercy's family's fault your life is what it is."

She recoils like a squirrel caught digging in the garbage. She knows how serious I am when it comes to defending Mercy. I know she doesn't mean any harm, but she can ramble on for hours when she's comparing herself to others or complaining about her life.

Mercy's mom has been nothing but kind to Mama and me. Sometimes she drops off cookies or loaves of bread with a little handwritten note, "You were on my heart today. God bless you." Mama will look annoyed at first, like she wants to know who has time to bake for other people. But then she rips off the plastic wrap and shoves the goodies straight into her mouth.

The last couple of months, Mama has needed a lot more attention. I think it's because of all the alcohol she's been drinking. At least that's what my heart is telling me. Because of it, I've started hiding out in my room with the door closed, writing in my own journal, trying to escape.

I wonder if reading Mama's journal is changing how I feel about her. Lately, I've been feeling a red hot flame of disgust for her. Maybe it's 'cause I'm frustrated with her living like she doesn't have one single thing to look forward to. No joy, no hope, no reason to put lipstick on. Every day is the same. She gets up, walks to the toilet to pee, walks down the hall to the kitchen to eat a little something, sometimes takes a shower, sometimes doesn't, gets dressed, wishes me a good day, hops in her truck and heads to the auto body shop, does some work, comes home, makes a simple supper, complains about the auto body shop, fills her special glass with wine, turns on the TV, and falls asleep on the couch as commercials roll in and out trying to sell a drunk woman the next best housecleaning product.

Most nights, when I come out of my room and try to wake her, she won't even move. The only thing that stirs her is turning off the TV.

"Velvet, now why'd you do that?"

Like she's been deeply invested in the program.

"You've been asleep for over an hour. I can't sleep with the TV on so loud. It's time for you to go to bed."

"Child, since when do you get to tell your mama when to go to bed?"

"Since you stopped putting yourself there."

Then Mama gets up like she was getting up anyway, goes to her room and shuts the door. I know she doesn't like me being the adult, but lately I've had to be. Every night I pray: *Lord, please help her see you so you can be the one to fill her up.*

It's no wonder Mama's life is like it is, really. She lost touch with nearly all of her friends from the Hip Joint. Most of them got married and had kids except for the twins, Debbie and Donna, who call every once in a while, hoping Mama will cross the tracks into Summerland and spend time like the good ol' days. I hear Mama on the phone saying, "No, no, I'm not up for it tonight."

She never seems to be up for it. But why? When is she gonna start living her life instead of waiting around for a man who clearly didn't care enough to stay?

There's a living, breathing man right here in Sack City who she sees at work every day and who I know still cares for her, Mr. Sullivan. Why isn't he good enough? Why doesn't she notice him? He's always good and kind her to her, but I guess good and kind aren't a part of how Mama measures the men she chooses.

I'm trying desperately not to have my own PLM moment, 'cause they aren't pretty, but everything Mama does and doesn't do is bugging me. Like the way she shouts "Velvet!" from the couch while I'm in my room with the door shut. I know she expects me to come running, but I ignore her. So she amps up her volume. "Vellll-vet!" Why can't she get up and come talk to me instead of yelling?

One of the things I love about Mercy is the way she accepts me without judgment. Father Matthew calls this unconditional love. Mercy sees the flaws in my family—well, in Mama—yet she accepts me the way I am. Mercy has been over after school and has witnessed firsthand Mama's PLM moments. It goes something like this:

Mercy, being as polite as she is, says, "How was your day, Miss Underwood?"

Mama, glass of wine already in hand, starts in about how hard her life is. "Well, you know, sweetheart, I have to work a full-time job 'cause I don't have a husband to help me pay for all of this."

Mama waves her hands around, making sure Mercy understands keeping up with our trailer home is hard work. I believe it is hard work, I do, especially since Pops died, because he used to help out a lot around the house. But I also believe Mama doesn't need to let the world know all of her troubles.

Mercy responds, "You sure do a fine job of taking care of your home."

Lately she has more patience for Mama than I do. She's always wanting to help out.

"Miss Underwood, is there anything I can get for you before I leave? Anything you want my family to pray for?" she asks sincerely.

Mama shakes her head no. "Thank you for asking, Mercy." I can tell Mama loves the attention Mercy gives her, and it makes me love Mercy even more.

I still haven't told Mercy about finding Mama's journal. I guess I'm feeling guilty about reading it and about keeping it all a secret. But I can't hold on to what I've read anymore. I need her to know.

Before school on Monday morning, I wait for Mercy by our special tree, spelling out my name in the dirt with the tip of my tennis shoe. What is taking her so long? I finally hear her humming and look up.

"Mercy, I've got to tell you something."

"What is it?" she asks, and I hesitate. "Well, what is it, Velvet?"

"Remember how I told you about my daddy being Diamond Jim? You know, the Strike Zone Champ from the bowling alley Hall of Fame wall?"

"Why yes, of course." Mercy hooks her arm into mine, and we walk slowly in the direction of the school.

"I found Mama's journal and it's all there. All of it!"

Mercy pauses, and her eyes get big.

"What happened to him? Where is he?" she asks.

"I haven't gotten to that part yet. I can only read it when Mama leaves the house, which isn't often. Or when she passes out. So far, I know how I came about ... you know, like how I was made!"

"Oh my goodness, Velvet!" She holds my arm even more tightly.

"I know he was somewhat of a ladies' man, you know, a flirt? And he and Mama were crazy about each other. I know Mrs. Evans also had a crush on him, which explains a lot! Anyway, I need to keep reading to find out what really happened—the truth about why he left."

"Do you need my help?"

"No, not yet. But maybe as I get more clues, I will."

"I have an idea!" Mercy stops walking and smiles at me. "Stay home from school one day. Pretend you're sick."

"Brilliant!" I say, though I don't like the idea of lying 'cause it makes me uncomfortable.

We arrive at school, and Mercy and I decide I'll be "sick" on Thursday. That way, I can be back at school on Friday to get any missed assignments and have the weekend to catch up. We both think this is such a good idea we jump up and down in the hallway. Janet walks by and looks at us. She has no idea what all the fuss is about, and I can tell that she'd like to by how she stares at us.

Mercy whispers, "Three more days until you figure out what happened to your daddy."

The thought of it makes me excited and nervous simultaneously, like when I have a stomach ache, but I still want to eat. I wonder if the journal is the port where my ship will finally come in.

Mama has no idea I'm up to something. On Tuesday, everything happens as usual. I get up for school, she gets up for work, and we go about our day. I feel guilty on Wednesday for not being attentive to Mama's needs lately, and that morning I offer to make her breakfast.

"I feel like eggs. Would you like some?" I ask.

Mama nods. "Sounds delicious."

I can't help but think I'll read the journal without interruption the next day. I clear my throat and ask for an aspirin.

"Are you sick, Velvet?" Mama looks worried.

"My throat is a little sore." I take a sip of orange juice and hold my throat.

Mama swirls her juice around the same way she does her wine and stares at me as I swallow.

"Now, don't go gettin' sick on me." She hands me an aspirin and ruffles my hair. "Ditty won't stop talking about bingo, and it looks like we both have to go on Thursday."

I swallow the pill with a giant gulp.

CHAPTER NINE
MARY

The day goes by quickly. After school, Mercy says, "Tomorrow is the big day! Are you ready to find out more?"

"I think so, but I'm nervous," I say.

"I wish I could miss school and be with you, but my parents make me go to school unless I'm throwing up or have a fever."

"I understand, and I wouldn't want you to get in any trouble."

Mercy and I approach our tree, and she squeezes my arm before she leaves.

"I'll stop by right after school to check on you before your mama gets home."

I nod yes, hoping I'm gonna have an awful lot to share with her.

"Don't forget to cough a lot!" Mercy giggles as she walks away.

As I get closer to home, I see the grotto Pops made for the 3-foot-tall Virgin Mary statue under the tree next to our garden. Mama hasn't kept up the yard or garden since Pops died, and soggy leaves from last fall are clumped around the statue's cracked and nubby feet. I walk toward her and push at the leaves with my shoes.

"Hello," I whisper.

It seems like yesterday I helped Pops set her up here in our front yard under the willow tree. Pops loved Mary. She was the only woman he ever put before Ditty, and Ditty never minded. She thought Mary was beautiful too, but she didn't ever join Pops on his Sunday trips to church. When I asked her why she'd say, "Sweetie, I think God hears me whether I'm sitting in an old wooden pew or right in here at this kitchen table."

I can't help but believe her. Mama is an on-again, off-again Catholic, and I guess I am a little of both of them combined. I see and feel God everywhere like Ditty, and I also love being in church, sitting at attention with my eyes closed and my heart open.

I can picture my younger self at church with Pops, waiting patiently on God to start talking. I'd sneak in a few words to make sure he knew I was ready: *It's me, Velvet. I'm here. Aisle three, sixth person in, purple dress.*

Funny thing about God, you can't hear him until he's good and ready. Father Matthew always says, "God's timing is different than ours."

When I was younger, I tried to wrap my head around that, but sometimes I just wanted what I wanted, when I wanted it.

I finish clearing away the leaves at Mary's feet then look straight into her eyes and whisper, "Please tell Pops hi from me."

When Mama comes home from work, I'm not at my usual spot at the kitchen table doing homework.

"Velvet?" she calls out.

"In here!" I say, from my bed. I clear my throat loudly and feel ashamed of myself. One minute ago, I was talking to the mother of Jesus, and now I'm lying to my own mother. I swear her journal is making me do things I wouldn't normally do. But I believe God understands. At least, I hope he does.

Mama stops in the doorway of my room. Her hair is in a messy bun, and she's holding her black high heels in her hand. She always dresses for work like she's selling cars instead of answering the phone and doing paperwork.

"Are you sick?" she asks.

"My throat hurts something fierce. I think I have a cold. Daniel sneezed and coughed all over me the other day in science, and I think he got me sick."

Mama shakes her head and mumbles something about Daniel's mom. "Well, try to rest in your room tonight. I'd hate for both of us to get it. Mikey wouldn't know what to do if I was out sick. Can I get you anything? Juice? An aspirin?"

Her attention to my needs makes me happy for a second, and then I feel even guiltier about lying. "No, no. I'm good right now but thank you. I'll stay in bed and rest." I pull the covers up closer to my chest. "Mama, do you remember when Pops put Mary in the yard?"

Mama smiles. "Yes, I sure do. Why do you ask?"

"Every time I see her, it makes me miss him, is all."

The phone rings, and Mama goes to the kitchen to answer it. I hear her tell Ditty I'm under the weather. I'm sure Ditty will head to the store to get everything for her homemade chicken noodle soup, and I'm not complaining. It's my favorite thing about being sick.

As expected, a few hours later, Ditty brings over the soup and even delivers it to me in bed on a special tray.

"I could get used to this," I say, sitting up. I remember I need to cough a little more.

"My sweet lil' Velvet ... I heard you weren't feeling good." Ditty puts her hand on my forehead. "No fever. That's good," she says.

I smile. "Thank you, Ditty. I'm sure this soup will help." (Cough! Cough!)

"Pops couldn't get enough of it. Sometimes I think he faked being sick, so I'd make it." Ditty winks at me and walks out of my room.

I eat a spoonful of soup and look out the window at the beat-up old garden, uncared for and unkempt, just like Mama's heart. I want Mama to come back to life in a big way, just like I want the garden to come back, without any weeds to get tangled up in like a sad past holding her back. I think about the arch and the rough edges of the grotto, and it occurs to me: Mama is like Mary in the grotto with her crumbling toes. All she needs is a firm foundation. Maybe if I could get her to church, it would help.

I burst into prayer: *Lord, thank you for Mary, Pops, Mama and Ditty. I will get Mama to church like Pops always wanted. I promise!*

Mama opens my door. "You best be getting to bed now." she says and takes the tray.

I pretend to cough and say, "OK." She pulls the covers up to my chin and kisses my forehead, and I feel sad for her. Not only does she miss her own daddy, whom she loved dearly, she also misses my daddy, whom she still loves.

"Why do you think Diamond Jim left us?"

As the weighted words fall from my lips, I look away.

"What makes you ask?" she says softly.

"I don't know. I guess I've been thinking, is all. Has he ever tried to find me?" I swallow hard like my throat hurts, but really, I want to cry.

"You get some rest now," she says. She turns out the lights and walks out of my room. So much for asking whatever I want about my daddy.

Suddenly, I want to hold Pops' handkerchief. I get up and open the top drawer of my dresser and search for the folded and ironed rectangle of worn cotton. I put it to my nose hoping to get a whiff of Pops, but it just smells like bleach and old wood. I get back in bed and stare at the moon shining on Mama's messy garden. I pray until I fall asleep like Pops taught me to do: *Hail Mary, full of grace ...*

CHAPTER 10
THURSDAY (FINALLY)

Thursday morning comes and my throat hurts from forcing fake coughs. Mama is already up and ready for work. *Thank you, Lord.* I decide to run a bath and stay in the tub until she leaves, so I won't have to make any eye contact. I cough every few minutes and moan like it hurts.

Mama knocks and peeks through the crack of the door. "Sounds like you're staying home sick from school today," she says. "I'll call the office and tell them."

I ask Mama to please get me a glass of juice and a cough drop and ask God again for his forgiveness.

"Do you need me to get you anything else?" Mama asks.

"No, I'll be fine. I'm gonna rest all day."

"OK then, I'll stop back a little later to check on you."

No, no, no! "Mama, you don't need to. I'll be fine."

She isn't used to me being sick. I never miss school. Ever.

"Stay at work," I say, a bit too eagerly, and produce another cough.

"OK. Ditty has her craft class today, but I'll let her know you're home sick. Her leftover soup is still in the fridge, if you want to warm it up later."

When I hear Mama's truck start, I jump out of the tub, grab Mama's peach robe from the hook on the door and go to her bedroom. I look outside to make sure she's gone. I cannot believe I pulled this off! I'm alone in the house with the truth about my daddy an arm's reach away.

I open the nightstand, and there's the journal, just like I left it. I climb onto Mama's unmade bed with it and find the pages before Mama found out she was pregnant:

I haven't written in a while. Since I met DJ, my life has been like a carnival ride, exciting and fast paced. For goodness' sakes, my cheeks hurt from grinning all the time. I've never been this happy! I love spending every possible moment with him. He makes me feel fulfilled and at peace, more so than I ever did with Mikey Sullivan. Nothing compares to DJ. We are always reaching for each other and touching, like magnets pulled by force until we connect in the middle.

Things seem to be getting pretty serious. We've been together for two whole months, and I'm certain we're falling in love. He comes to the Hip Joint every night I dance, and afterwards we sit at the bar and talk for hours. DJ makes me feel the way I do when I'm dancing— like no one can break me. He's always telling me I'm beautiful and sexy and talented. He compliments every dance routine saying, "You were the best one on stage tonight, Lynette," kissing my neck and making me ache for him. I guess it's why I end up in his arms at the end of every night. His charm is impossible to resist. There's no

*one in this town like DJ, and frankly, there's no one like
me either. We're a perfect pair.*

*The women of Sack City don't know how to handle
me. They get all wound up when they realize they don't
have the kind of confidence I do. Ditty and Pops always
say I'm a firework meant for a big open sky. I used to
wonder why on earth I chose to stay in Sack City, where
fireworks can't even be sold. But now I know, God kept
me here so I could meet the love of my life, David James,
Diamond Jim, my DJ.*

*The second the single girls figured out he was here to
stay, they started showing up like coyotes sniffing around
at night, hoping to sink their teeth into him. One of 'em
is Joan Evans, who's been hanging around the Hip Joint
more and more. I told DJ about how she tried out to be a
dancer but didn't make the cut, which irritated her to no
end. He said she seems like a real nice lady, and I acted
like it didn't bother me. But I know Joan well enough to
know her nice lady act is a ploy to get something that
belongs to me.*

*Tonight, as I was getting ready to go on stage for my
set, I peeked at the bar and noticed Joan sidled up to
DJ. I asked Debbie if she'd dance the next set. When she
asked why, I told her I was about to put that conniving
Joan Evans in her place. She told me to be careful and
wished me good luck.*

*As the lights went dim and everyone turned toward
the stage, I watched as Joan reached for some peanuts
at the bar and brushed her hand across DJ's arm. How*

could DJ let her get so close to him? I've never felt jealousy before. I never had to. Mikey Sullivan only had eyes for me. This was a new feeling. Who does Joan think she is, anyway? She knows damn well DJ is mine. She always seems to have a thing for the men who like me. The moment she knew Mikey had a crush on me, she made sure he noticed her. "Hi, Mikey," and "You sure look good in those jeans, Mikey." Always flirting and trying to get between us. Why? I guess everyone has their enemies, and she chose me.

My first instinct was to walk right up to the bar and make myself known. Instead, I stood in a shadowy corner of the club like an alley cat in the dark and watched them. Joan leaned in, smiled and whispered something to DJ. He smiled back. When Debbie was halfway through her set, DJ asked Jimmy for two beers and slid one over to Joan. They clinked their bottles together like they were celebrating. My blood started to boil. I couldn't stand it anymore. I had to confront them.

"I hate to interrupt you two," I said.

They set their beers down at the same time. Joan looked shocked for a moment and then picked up her beer and took a long, slow sip like she could make me disappear. Then she stood up, winked at DJ and said, "Y'all have a good night now, ya hear?"

I grabbed a hold of her arm and got real close. She looked panicked, told me to let go, and asked if I was out of my mind. I warned her if she kept trying to get close to my man, she would see crazy.

As all this was happening, DJ didn't say anything. Joan was smirking like she didn't have a care in the world. So I continued to stare her down, forcing her to look away first. Then she walked off without another word.

DJ pulled me in close and asked, "What was all that about, pretty lady?" I wanted to ask him right then and there why he let her get so close to him, but I didn't. I didn't mention I'd seen him buy her a beer. Why on earth didn't I say something? My blood was still boiling, but his hands around my waist calmed me and made the image of Joan Evans touching his arm disappear.

"Look here," he said, taking my chin in his hand and drawing me in deeper with his eyes. He said if he wanted that redheaded hussy, he would have run after her, but he didn't. He was right there with me. I think he liked how fired up I was about the two of them talking. I think it made him feel important. He forced a smile out of me, and before I knew it, we were in the parking lot of the Hip Joint, kissing in his car. In fact, Joan's little escapade stirred up jealously in me that resulted in some fast-paced making out. I yanked DJ's shirt over his head, exposing his bare chest. My hands and mouth explored his body. I wanted him to know without a doubt he had the best woman in town. Judging by his groaning, he agreed 100 percent. We ended up making love right in the parking lot.

Mama! No! Ew! I throw the journal away from me like it's

a hot potato. It lands on the floor near the bathroom door. I'm never gonna be able to look at the parking lot of what is now the Suds 'n' Duds Laundromat the same way again. I close my eyes and say a prayer: *Lord, please forgive Mama! And I hope you'll forgive me, too. I know it's strange for me to be reading about this stuff. But if it's OK with you, I'm gonna keep reading. If for some reason I shouldn't, please send me a sign.*

I open my eyes and wait a few minutes. Nothing happens. I get up off the bed and pick up the journal. No lights flicker. No thunderous noises rumble from above. I guess God thinks it's OK, so I settle back into reading:

I'm going to bed tonight with a huge smile on my face. Come to think of it, I'll bet DJ is too! I know all the girls at the Hip Joint think he's a ladies' man, and after seeing him and Joan tonight, I do wonder a little. But tonight was mostly Joan's fault. The girls only see trouble, but I see a man who's falling in love with me! Even Pops likes him! Ditty has her reservations, but that's just because she doesn't know what we have. I found a good man! I pray every night, thanking the good Lord for bringing DJ into my life.

I don't understand Mama. She had her suspicions and just ignored them. But why? Because she didn't want to lose him?

I carry the journal to the kitchen and set it on the table. I melt some butter in a pan and break open two eggs. Ditty taught me how to make perfect fried eggs by keeping the heat on low and covering the skillet with a lid. After I eat my perfect eggs, I look out the window. Even in the daylight I notice the light outside our front door flickering on and off, and it makes me miss Pops. He used to be over all the time fixing things.

"Hey, Pops, our porch light doesn't want to turn on. I replaced the bulb, but nothing is happening," I remember Mama telling him.

Pops stood tall, proud to have been asked to fix something. "Hmm, well, let me take a look at it."

Mama went to work, and I went to school while Pops spent hours fiddling with wires. When we came home, we were delighted to see the light shining brightly.

"My goodness!" Mama stopped in her tracks. "He has gone and fixed the light, Velvet." She walked in and flipped the switch up and down, but the light wouldn't turn off. "Hmm," she said. "I'm sure he'll be by later to brag about his handiwork, and I'll ask why it won't turn off."

Sure enough, he and Ditty rolled into the driveway a short time later, honking the horn to let us know they'd arrived. I ran and jumped into Pops' arms. Mama said, "Thanks for fixing the light, Pops."

Pops puffed up like a peacock. If he'd had feathers, they'd have been unapologetically spreading in glorious color. "Well, it took me a few hours, but I finally got it," he said.

"The only thing is, we can't seem to get the darn thing to turn off," Mama said.

"Oh, you'll need to go to the electrical panel next to the bathroom and unscrew the fuse I marked 'front light' for you."

Ditty shook her head. "Lord, have mercy. You're gonna set the house on fire."

"That easy, huh, Pops?" Mama looked at me and Ditty, and we all laughed.

"What's so funny?" Pops asked. He'd probably worked for hours without taking a break to get the darn light to work for us. It didn't matter to him that it couldn't be turned on and off with the switch like it used to; the light worked and that was enough.

Mama never did unscrew the fuse to turn off the light, so it stayed on day and night, and Mama just replaced the light bulb whenever it burned out. Pops told everyone in town he fixed the light and bragged that he was available for hire as an electrician, if need be. Ditty would whisper to the nearest person, "It's a wonder he hasn't burned the whole town down."

I bet it broke Pops' heart when Diamond Jim left Mama and me. That's probably why he spent so much time at our house fixing things and lending a hand.

The phone on the wall rings and jolts me back to reality. "Hello?" I answer.

"How are you feeling?" Mama asks.

"I'm good Mama." I remember to cough. "My throat is still sore, but I'm resting and reading."

Shoot! I told her I was reading! I hope she doesn't ask me what I'm reading. Is she ever worried I might find the journal and read it? It's not like she's really hiding it.

"I told Mikey I may have to leave early 'cause you're sick and all."

I gulp. "Mama, stay at work. I'm fine. Really. No sense in you getting behind at work on account of me." *Lord, keep her at work.*

"OK. Maybe read less so you can rest more."

"Yes, Mama."

I look up at the creamy ceiling and ask God once again for forgiveness as I go back to the journal and read the next entry:

Being Diamond Jim's woman is like a full-time job, and one that I love, but it's beginning to take a toll on me. Between dancing at the Hip Joint and our dates and late nights together, I'm exhausted. So when DJ told me a few days ago he was going to visit his daddy and would be gone for the weekend, I was relieved at the thought of getting some much-needed sleep.

The day he left, he said, "I'm gonna miss you, Lynette Underwood." His lips found mine and he held on to me like he didn't want to leave. Then he asked me to come with him! I smiled at the sentiment, but I had to work. We gave each other one more long, passionate kiss, he slid into the front seat of his Cadillac, unrolled the window, smiled up at me and said, "See you in a few days, baby." I wanted to tell him I loved him, but I didn't say the words. I waved and blew him a kiss as he drove off.

As I walked back toward the house, I felt a tinge of nausea and paused. I took a few deep breaths and made my way to the door. The nausea kept building, so I ran straight to the sink and threw up. Just then, Ditty walked in the door humming a tune. I felt weak and my skin felt clammy as I turned to look at her. She stopped in her

tracks when she saw me at the sink. "Lynette Lucille,
YOU'RE PREGNANT!"

CHAPTER 11
PREGNANT

I try to hold the journal still, but my hands are shaking. Mama was pregnant with me! I almost rip the page as I turn it too fast. Mama wrote:

I knew Ditty was right. I hadn't gotten my period in two months. I told myself it was 'cause of all the excitement of being in a new relationship. I kept thinking it would come any day, since DJ and I have settled into a nice routine.

Ditty followed me into my bedroom wanting answers. I told her it was something I ate, but she didn't believe me. She said, "Please! I had the same green look on my face when I was pregnant with you. What on earth were you thinking, letting that snake of a traveling salesman knock you up?"

I snapped at Ditty, "He's not a snake!" I wanted to say more, but I couldn't think of anything else. She hasn't witnessed the tenderness he shows me. There is so much more to DJ.

Ditty went on lecturing me, saying if I had stayed

with Mikey this never would have happened. She wanted to know how a girl like me, with the sweetest daddy on earth, managed to get involved with someone like Diamond Jim. I knew Ditty wasn't thrilled about DJ, but she doesn't really know him. In her mind, she had me married to Mikey Sullivan a long time ago. And I get it. Mikey is a lot like Pops, always fixing things and helping people. Ditty and Pops watched Mikey and me grow up together. Mikey is great and all, but he's not my DJ.

Ditty continued to swirl around me, making me dizzy. "I have no idea what we'll tell Pops," she said.

I hadn't thought about Pops, but then again, I haven't thought about anyone but DJ since the day I met him. I felt like I was letting everyone down. Even DJ.

Ditty insisted on taking me to see Dr. Dearberg right away. In the car, she put her hand on my leg and let me know he was a kind man who would keep everything private. My stomach swished as Ditty turned out of the driveway, and I closed my eyes and prayed.

The doctor's office was inside a white house with a black sign above the front door that read JIM DEARBERG, M.D. Dr. Dearberg lived upstairs, and his practice was on the main level. He had one nurse who doubled as his receptionist. Ditty waited by the entrance for me to get out of the car, but I couldn't move. I didn't want to know. It hadn't even been an hour since I'd said goodbye to DJ. I imagined he was well on his way, singing with the windows down, my kiss still on his lips.

Ditty marched back to the car and told me I needed

to be brave. I nodded as tears streamed down my cheeks. I knew I didn't need a test. All the signs were there. I should have been more careful, used some form of birth control. But Sack City is such a small town, I think I was afraid everyone would find out. Especially Ditty, who wanted me to wait for the right man (Mikey). Now look at me. Ditty and Pops will be so ashamed.

Why did I believe DJ when he said, "I always get it right"? I hear Jenny's voice in my head saying, "He told you what? Oh, Lynette. I told you he was a ladies' man. He flat out lied to you."

Ditty marched back and opened the car door. I wiped away tears and followed her into the doctor's office. Ditty spoke to the nurse, and we took a seat in the waiting area. Moments later, after I peed in a cup and handed it back to the nurse, I was in the exam room. Dr. Dearberg did a pelvic exam and asked me about my last period, if I was sexually active, and if I'd been using birth control. I told him my boyfriend used the "rhythm method." All the while, he scribbled notes in my chart. Then he said, "We won't have your test results back for a couple of weeks, but based on what you've just told me, it appears you're eight to 10 weeks pregnant."

I avoided his eyes and searched for patterns in the speckled linoleum floor instead.

Dr. Dearberg wanted to know if I had any questions. I asked if throwing up and being tired all the time were normal for pregnant women. He said yes, for some. I struggled to get my next question out: "What if I don't want to keep the baby?"

My reading comes to a halt. I can't believe it. My eyes go over Mama's words again. "What if I don't want to keep the baby?" My heart pounds and my whole body shakes. *Lord? I don't know what else to say. I'm here, she kept me, but why?*

I want to feel normal again, so I put my jacket on and go outside to the garden, and to Mary. The old, wet leaves have made their way back to her feet. This time I scoop them all into my arms and carry them to the garbage can. Back in the garden, I pull up one of the green buds that's poking through the soil, bulb and all—a gift for Mary. My foot gets stuck on an unruly vine, and I trip. Something about being in the wake of Mama's past makes me feel heavy.

I walk the plant back to Mary in the grotto, dig a hole with my bare hands, and push the bulb deep into the earth. Maybe nurturing this new life will help. I step back and look at Mary and the bud. I don't say a prayer. I don't know what to say. I stand there with my dirty hands at my sides. The tears begin to come. My thoughts are all over the place. Where is my daddy? Why is he such a coward? Why wasn't Mama more careful? What did Pops say? I'm on my knees now. The tears drop so fast and so furious, the dirt on my hands turns to mud.

I hear footsteps and turn to see Mercy running toward me.

"Are you OK?" She kneels beside me and holds me tight.

"Mercy, Mama didn't want me. She didn't want me at all."

"It's gonna be all right. Shhh now, Velvet. It's gonna be all right," Mercy says as she wipes my tears.

"I don't want to read it anymore. Not now, not ever," I say.

"I understand, I do. But what if there's more? I mean, you're here now, aren't you? Don't you want to find out why?"

I look at Mary and the bright green bud at her feet and somehow find the strength to stand. Mercy grabs my hand, and we walk back to the house. I wash up in the kitchen sink. We go down the hall to Mama's room together.

Mercy picks up the journal from Mama's bed. "Show me where you left off." She flips through the pages of Mama's life like she's looking through a comic book. "Wow, there's a lot of stuff written in here."

I point to where it says, "What if I don't want to keep the baby?" The shame Mama must have felt rises up in me. "See Mercy, she's talking about me."

Mercy scoots closer to me and looks me in the eye. "Velvet, it was OK for her to be afraid. People say and do things they wouldn't normally say or do when they're afraid."

I know she's right. So why is this breaking my heart?

I read aloud to Mercy:

Dr. Dearberg wanted to know if I had any questions. I asked if throwing up and being tired all the time were normal for pregnant women. He said yes, for some. I struggled to get my next question out: "What if I don't want to keep the baby?"

He said I had some big decisions to make. What did he mean? Having the baby? Giving it up for adoption? Or was he talking about abortion? I didn't have the nerve to ask since abortion is against the law. Jenny told me about some doctors in big cities who are willing to perform illegal abortions for the right price, so I made a mental note to ask her privately. Finally, Dr. Dearberg said, "I can see this was not in your plan and you have a lot of questions. Why don't we schedule another exam in two weeks? We'll have your test results by then, and you can discuss it with the baby's father in the meantime."

I didn't catch everything he said after "the baby's father." Those words hung in the air. What was I going to tell DJ? As the doctor rambled on about reliable methods of birth control, he must've known my thoughts were elsewhere. He coughed and said, "My dear, the rhythm method is not a reliable form of birth control."

I stop reading, and Mercy and I look at each other.

"The rhythm method? What is it?" Mercy asks.

My mind goes back to health class. "Remember when we learned about reproduction? The man's you-know-what goes in the girl's pocketbook, and he does his thing …" Mercy's eyes widen. "… all I can think is there's some sort of rhythm to it."

Not knowing the answer, we sit silent for a few seconds. I go back to reading out loud:

The conversation with Dr. Dearberg ended with him saying abstinence is always best. But it will take superhuman powers to abstain from Diamond Jim. My flesh is weak when it comes to him.

I left the exam room to find Ditty thumbing through a magazine in the waiting room. She gave me a knowing glance, and we walked to the car without saying a word. As she drove, I put my hand out the window, pretending nothing was wrong. Ditty tried to talk to me, but I didn't respond, I just wanted to be alone. I closed my eyes as the damp August air floated between my fingers.

Mercy looks at me. "See, Velvet? She needed some time to think about it. She comes to her senses. I mean, I'm staring at you, ain't I? So it all has to work out."

For the first time, Mercy's optimism doesn't work. "Except the daddy part," I say. "That part doesn't work out." More tears come, and I'm not sure how to handle what's inside the pages of Mama's journal. It's all too real now, too heavy. I try to think of reasons to stop reading. "Soon DJ's gonna find out about me and make the decision to leave."

Mercy reaches for my hand.

"I think we should stop reading for the day," I say. "I'll let you know if I get back to it. But Mama's gonna be home soon."

Mama pulls into the driveway, and Mercy and I look at each other and scream. The journal flies into the air and lands face down on the carpet. We hear Mama's car door close. Mercy grabs the journal. I'm frozen in place.

"Where does it go?" Mercy asks, waving the journal around, not knowing what to do with it.

I open the nightstand drawer, and she throws it inside like it's the hottest thing she's ever touched with her bare hands. We both run to the living room as Mama enters the house.

"Velvet, I'm home!" Mama announces.

Mercy and I look like we've been caught stealing. Mercy

starts talking nervously. "Hi, Miss Underwood. I stopped by
to check on Velvet, 'cause she's sick and all. She seems better.
Right, Velvet?"

I nod yes. I can't look at Mama.

"Anyhoo, I've got to get home now. I wanted to give Velvet
the assignments she missed today." Mercy looks around and
sees there are no notebooks or papers out, and it only makes her
more nervous. "They're in her room. Well, OK then. Bye. I'll
see you tomorrow at our tree, Velvet."

I wave goodbye to Mercy and walk to my room. I don't want
to talk to Mama, but she follows me anyway.

"Is Mercy OK? She was acting kinda funny."

"Yep, she's fine."

"Is your cough better? It's unusual for a cough to have such
a short duration."

I'm not even concerned by her curiosity. "Seems to be," I
say.

"Well then, are you up for bingo tonight?"

"I'll think about it. I have a lot of schoolwork to catch up
on." I look up to see if she's turning to leave, but she's standing
there looking at me.

"Is everything OK, Velvet? Anything you want to talk
about?"

As a matter of fact, yes! I'd like to talk about the fact you
were reckless, selfish and didn't even want your own baby!

"Nope, I'm all good." But I'm not. I'm terrible.

Ditty phones and must be asking Mama if I'm well enough
to go to bingo, because I hear Mama say, "I don't think so,"

and then, "Sure … I need to see if Velvet's all right. Something seems off."

Ditty arrives like clockwork with her pregame pork chops and applesauce. She knocks on my door, even though it's wide open. "Hi, sweetie. How you feeling today?"

"OK." I look up at her and try to smile.

"The ladies will be disappointed if you're not at bingo tonight."

I think what Ditty is really saying is that she'll be sad if I don't go. It's the best feeling I've had all day.

"I have a lot of homework to catch up on, being I was sick." I muster a baby cough. "You two go and have fun."

"How 'bout you join us for dinner, at least? I'll call you when it's ready." She gives me her sweet smile.

"OK," I say. She'd hate if I didn't enjoy her meal.

When Ditty leaves my room, I look out my window and a prayer pours out: *God, it hasn't been the greatest day for me. I've done a lot of lying to both Mama and Ditty. Mercy even had to lie a little bit too. What I read made me so sad. Help me to see the peak of the mountain that comes after you've been in the valley. I know only you can help. I know you will. Is Mama still in the valley? It's so hard for me to know. I love you.*

When Ditty calls for dinner, I sit down at the table, and they both stare long and hard at me. I act like I don't notice. I cut into my pork chop and dip it in the applesauce. Mama gets up to get me a glass of milk.

"I didn't ask for milk," I snap.

"You usually love milk with dinner." Mama gives Ditty a puzzled look.

I realize I'm being rude. "Sorry. No, it's fine. Thank you."

Mama and Ditty start a conversation, and it takes their attention off me. When Ditty mentions "Ol' Doc Dearberg is ill and has been for some time," my head snaps up to see Mama's reaction. Her eyes have a faraway look, like she's back in the moment I read about hours before.

"That's terrible news. He's a kind man."

Mama thinks Dr. Dearberg is kind? How did he help her? I need to get back to the journal.

"Was he the doctor who delivered me?" I ask fearlessly.

"Why, yes he was." Mama smiles at Ditty.

The second they leave for bingo, I head back to Mama's bedroom. This time, I sit on the floor with my back firmly against the wall. I go to the next entry in the journal:

DJ finally called. When he greeted me with his usual, "Hello there, beautiful," I pushed my cheek into the phone wanting desperately to be close to him. He told me he'd been missing me, and I gripped the phone tighter. It felt like a lifetime ago we'd kissed goodbye in my driveway—before the throwing up, before the peeing in the cup, before Dr. Dearberg said, "It appears you're pregnant." But DJ didn't know any of it, and I wasn't ready to tell him. Not over the phone. So instead, I told him I hadn't been feeling well and I was missing him too. He responded, "I'm gonna stay here a few more days. I hope you feel better soon, 'cause when I get back, I'm going to take you for a drive." I knew instantly what he meant, and normally it would have sent an electric shock straight through my body. This time, it just made me sad. I told him I'd see him soon and hung up, wondering if anything was ever going to be the same again.

I move on to the journal entry from the next day:

I woke up at 2:30 this morning with severe cramping. I ran to the bathroom, and when I pulled my underpants down, they were covered in blood. I didn't know why I was bleeding, I thought I wasn't supposed to get my period. The cramps kicked in again. They were different than normal period cramps. They wrapped tightly around my back and radiated pain through the middle of my belly. It was so bad I screamed and doubled over. I sat down on the toilet and felt something slide out of me and into the water. The cramps stopped. My whole body shook as I looked at the blood and clots in the toilet. I scooped it up with the water glass next to the sink, my hand trembling. I stared at it. I knew it was my baby. Our baby.

The baby wasn't me! Mama lost the baby. She was pregnant and then just like that she wasn't. Why did God take her baby? All day I've been thinking Mama didn't want me. *Forgive me, Lord. What did Mama do with the baby? Is my brother or sister in heaven with Pops? Did Mama tell DJ the baby died?* I go back to reading the journal with a racing heart and tears in my eyes:

I called Ditty and asked her to come over immediately. She started asking all sorts of questions until I said, "Come over, Mama. I need you." I never call her Mama anymore, only Ditty. The second I did, she hung up the phone. Ten minutes later, she was standing in my bedroom. I told her I lost the baby, and she asked if I was OK. I pointed to the glass next to the bathroom sink, and my eyes filled with tears. She sat next to me and said, "Let's take this to Dr. Dearberg as soon as his office opens. I'm sure he'll want to have a look at you, to make sure everything is OK." But nothing is OK.

I haven't told DJ about the baby—now what will I say? "Hey honey, I have some news. I was pregnant and now I'm not. We had a baby and now we don't." I couldn't stop crying, so Ditty just held me tight. She said she hadn't told Pops either and asked if I wanted her to. I told her no one else needed to know. She asked if I wanted her to take the glass with her, to get it out of the house so I could rest. I told her no, I didn't want to be separated from my baby. She assured me what happened to me happens often to women. "There's not always a rhyme or reason to it, Lynette. Sometimes the body doesn't take the baby." She added, "Next time, you can get pregnant the proper way."

That was not what I wanted to hear. God taking the baby made me feel cheated. I wanted to make the decision myself. All this time, I'd been thinking I didn't want a baby, but I hadn't made up my mind. What if I'd decided to keep it after all? What if DJ had wanted to be a daddy? What if he and I were about to start our lives as a family? I pictured the three of us pulling up to church in DJ's Caddy, the whole town oohing and aahing over how sweet our little family was. But Ditty quickly brought me back to reality—told me to be more careful and wait for DJ to propose to me. I couldn't find the words to respond. I was numb.

I press the journal against my heart. If Mama fell in love with this child, then surely, she wanted me. Of course, she did. I could keep reading, but it's been a long day. I put the journal back in the drawer. I am loved, and maybe even wanted, by both Mama and DJ. I feel lighter as I get ready for bed.

Mama comes home from bingo and checks in on me. "Velvet!" she says in a loud whisper. "I won a hundred dollars at bingo tonight! Did you hear me?"

I'm half asleep, but I manage to say, "That's wonderful, Mama. I'm so happy for you." And I am.

"You should have been there, Velvet."

"Mama, can I have a hug?"

Mama steps over to my bed. She smells like cigarettes and root beer, the same way Ditty and I smell on bingo nights. I reach for her, and she squeezes me tight.

"I love you, Mama."

"I love you too, sugar. Now we need to decide how we're gonna celebrate this big win."

I smile at the word "we."

CHAPTER 12

JESUS AND BOBBY JOHNSON

I wake the next morning smiling, a dream fresh in my thoughts. It was so real I want to stay in bed. I sit up and look out my window, taking a moment to remember, and write it all down in my journal.

In the dream, I was walking down a narrow path, and on either side bunches of pretty yellow flowers reached out in every direction. I knew the path was leading me toward someone, but I had no idea who. I took my time, turning my head from side to side, greeting the sun-colored blossoms. As I got farther along, the path began to wind, and the golden blooms were more plentiful. I'd never seen such beauty.

I heard someone humming and then a giggle. I wanted to get closer, so I ran. As I did, the flowers swayed as if they were cheering me on. I could see a warm bright light ahead and a clear blue sky. And that's when I saw them: Jesus (it looked like him from the pictures, white robe, long hair) and a giggling little boy with Mama's eyes. They were sitting on a wooden swing under a big blooming tree, and they both smiled at me.

"Velvet," Jesus said as he reached out for me. "We're so glad you came."

The second my hand was about to meet his, I woke up.

I can't stop grinning. But who was the little boy? I feel the need to draw, and I search in my stash of markers until the yellow one appears. I draw a yellow flower and then another and another until I fill the whole page with dancing wild blossoms. I try to draw the winding path, the tree and the swing, but it doesn't come close to the beauty I experienced.

Mama opens my door. "Velvet, how come you aren't up yet? Are you feeling OK?"

I forget for a second I played sick yesterday. "Mama, I had a such a special dream."

Mama opens my door a little wider. Some people don't like to hear about other people's dreams, but Mama loves them. She says there are signs in them. "Well, what was it? We ain't got all day, young lady."

"There was a path with yellow flowers, and at the end of the path, guess who was waiting to meet me?"

"Elvis?"

I can't help but laugh. "No, Mama! Not Elvis. It was Jesus!" I can't hide my excitement. I hold up the picture I drew.

From the doorway, Mama squints at the flowers. "Lord have mercy, Velvet. You're losing it." She starts to close the door.

"Mama, Jesus wasn't alone. There was a little boy with him. A giggling little boy." Mama stands still. Frozen, like a memory has seized her heart. "Mama? Did you hear me?"

Her shoulders fall and for a second she looks lost in a thought. "Sounds like a lovely dream."

She fishes in the pocket of her robe for her cigarettes and tells me more about bingo and her big win. Mr. Sullivan was at the bingo hall with his mama, and Ditty kept whispering to Mama how handsome he was. I try to pay attention, but I don't care about any of it. When Mama finally leaves my room, I get ready quickly 'cause I need to get to Mercy. I need to tell her the baby Mama wrote about in her journal wasn't me, that she didn't want to get rid of me after all.

Even though I'm in a hurry, when I see Mary outside, I stop. The bud I planted needs water. A little rainwater has collected in the watering can by the shed, so I pour it on the plant. While I do, I think about Mama's child who didn't survive.

"Please tell the baby I'm sorry," I say to Mary. "Tell it I'm sure Mama would have loved it." I try to imagine what the baby would look like. Would it have dark hair and big brown eyes, like Diamond Jim—a mini Strike Zone Champ—or would it look more like Mama and me, with blue-green eyes and brown hair?

I glance toward our tree to see if Mercy is close. She gets there before me, and I wave frantically as I make my way toward her.

"Velvet, what took you so long? What else did you find out?"

I grab her shoulders and look into her eyes. "You aren't gonna believe this, Mercy! The baby, the one we thought was me, it wasn't me at all."

Mercy's mouth is wide open, and her eyes are about to pop out of her head. Other kids walk past us on their way to school. "Velvet, what do you mean, it wasn't you?" Mercy looks me up and down.

"The baby Mama was pregnant with, it didn't make it. Mama had a miscarriage."

"Oh my sweet Lord. I can't believe what you're saying right now. The baby, the one she wasn't sure she wanted, it died?"

"While Mama was at bingo last night, I read more, and I'm glad I did. I have a sibling in heaven, Mercy. A baby bro ..."

I stop before the words come out of my mouth and goose bumps rise on my arms. I picture Mama's face when I told her about my dream.

Mercy says, "Your poor mama. She lost a baby and your daddy." She pulls my arm to keep moving, but I can't get the image of the giggling little boy out of my head. We get closer to school and Mercy is still talking. "This means your mama is gonna get pregnant again! With you! And this time, we'll find out what really happened!"

I want to tell Mercy about the dream, but there's not enough time before we get to school. So I blurt out, "Mercy, I had a dream about a baby boy. And Jesus was there too."

"You had a dream about Jesus and a baby boy?" She fits all the pieces together and stops in her tracks. She turns to face me. "Oh, Velvet! God was trying to tell you something! You have a brother in heaven!"

Sitting in Mrs. Holden's class, I try to focus on school, but all I can do is draw flowers and think about the dream. I wonder what happened to the baby. Did Mama bury him? Did Dr. Dearberg keep him in his office?

Mrs. Johnson's grandson, Bobby, interrupts my thoughts. "Excuse me, Velvet," he says. I'm so lost in Mama's past I don't even look at him. "Can I borrow a pencil?"

I finally come to. Did Bobby Johnson ask to borrow a pencil?

I stop drawing, look up, and force a smile, but I think I may look more annoyed than happy. I'm not though. Just shocked, I guess.

When Bobby and I were kids, we gravitated toward each other, playing tag and chasing bugs between my yard and his grandma's. Heck, I remember our dirty knees knocking against each other's while we ate Popsicles on his grandma's front steps. But growing up has a way of changing the way you are with someone, and ever since we became teenagers, being ourselves has been hard to do. Like our past disappeared and we have to start over. Truth is, I don't really know Bobby Johnson anymore. At least, that's what it feels like.

But now I notice everything about him: his dimples; his eyes, which are a soft blue like the water at the public pool on a hot summer night; the way he stands with one knee slightly bent; the way he squints when the teacher asks him a question. I try to focus. For goodness' sakes, the boy asked to borrow a pencil! Calm down, Velvet. But my stomach twists and turns. This must be what butterflies feel like?

Bobby gives me my pencil back after class. "Thanks, Velvet. Did you understand what Mrs. Holden was talking about?"

"No, not really." I'm blushing, I know it. This is more than he's said to me all year. I look around to see if anybody else is seeing what I'm seeing. Bobby walks away, and I stare at the back of the boy I used to know. He used to be a pudgy little kid, and one summer his shoulders got strong and steady. Mama has said she fell in love with Diamond Jim 'cause his shoulders looked like he had the strength to hold her up.

Sandra Shaw walks toward me after class, her tan plaid skirt swaying from side to side. She looks determined, like she's mad and about to punch me in the nose. The clip-clop of her shoes gets louder as she gets closer and stops as she plants her penny loafers by my locker.

"Bobby Johnson has a crush on you, and I thought you should know."

"Me?"

"Yes, you! I heard him talking to his friends at the vending machine."

Bobby is standing with his friends. Do I dare make eye contact? As quickly as I think it, our eyes lock. Oh no! Why did I look so soon? I divert my eyes and look at anything other than Bobby Johnson. They land on the quote of the day on the hallway bulletin board. It's from Albert Einstein: "A person who never made a mistake never tried anything new." I'm already making mistakes! I wish I never looked. I mean, what does Sandra Shaw know anyway? Why would I trust her?

"OK, thanks," I say.

"You should also know, Janet has a crush on him." Sandra says. She spins on her loafers and walks away.

I close my locker and look in Bobby's direction again. Thankfully, he's getting something out of his locker and doesn't see me looking. I need Mercy. Now!

In my mind, I replay what just happened. I can't figure out if Sandra was warning me or informing me. The bell stops ringing and I walk past Bobby without a glance to Mercy's locker. She takes her own sweet time getting there, and my eyes dart up and down the hallway while I pray for her to hurry up. That's when I see her talking to Bobby's best friend, Tommy. I mean, what are the chances? What are they talking about? I can sense Mercy is hurrying through the conversation 'cause she keeps looking in my direction, and her smile is so big I can't help but smile in anticipation.

"You aren't going to believe this!" Mercy says, jogging toward me.

"Mercy, I have something to tell you! Something you're not going to believe, either. Bobby Johnson has a crush on me!"

At the same time she says, "Bobby Johnson has a crush on you! His best friend just told me! And Velvet, they want us to go the movies on Saturday night."

"Like a date?" I ask.

"Yes, but not really a date. More like a we'll all-just-happen-to-be-at-the-same-movie kinda thing."

I nod like I understand, but I don't. My stomach gets queasy, and my palms start to sweat. "I don't know if I wanna go on a date that's not really a date. I don't even know how to do that, Mercy."

"You're freaking out, but you don't need to. It will be real casual. Velvet?"

Mercy can tell I'm stuck in my head. This is all too new. Too fast.

"OK," I say reluctantly, "But I'm nervous. He's in my science class, last period. What am I supposed to do? Why does Bobby Johnson like me all of a sudden? I know Tommy will tell him you and him talked about the date. Oh my word, this is going to be so awkward." I squeeze my books against my chest.

"Be normal, Velvet!"

Normal? What does normal even mean anymore?

Mercy and I get in line for lunch. It's beef stroganoff, but I think I'm too nervous or excited to eat it. The lunch lady slops the saucy noodles on my tray and adds a spoonful of broccoli and a carton of milk. Mercy and I find a seat. I see Sandra whispering to Janet, and they're both looking directly at me.

"Mercy," I lean in to whisper, "Sandra said Janet likes Bobby, too."

"Lord, have mercy." I've never heard Mercy use her name like that. She looks around for Janet. "Don't pay her no mind. She's jealous."

It's hard not to compare myself with Janet. She's polished, like she's put in the kind of hard work Mama's always talking about. "Velvet, if you want a man to notice you, you gotta spend some time on yourself." I picture Mama putting on red lipstick, like she used to before a show. I'm sure Janet Evans studies the Sears catalog for just the right thing to buy, and Mrs. Evans makes sure her daughter gets exactly what she wants.

I look at the catalog too, but for me it's more like dreaming than studying. Will I have to wear lipstick to school now? I can't compete with Janet. I don't even want to try.

"I don't get it, Mercy."

"You don't get what?"

"Why would Bobby like me if Janet Evans likes him?"

"Now, you stop right there, Velvet Mary. You are prettier, kinder and a heck of a lot sweeter."

"Thank you." I smile, secretly wishing I believed her.

The bell rings, and I haven't even gone to my locker yet to switch my books. Bobby and Tommy walk past us, and I hold my breath. They don't say a word, thank God! Is this going to be my life now—awkward and breathless?

Before I know it, it's nearly the end of the day and time for science. I wait for the very last second to enter class. If I get there too early, Bobby might say something to me, and I'm afraid I won't know what to say back. Sandra Shaw is in class too, and I'm afraid she'll start something about me and Bobby. Me and Bobby. Oh boy, that sounds strange. Sandra has a reputation for starting rumors, like the one she spread about her own best friend, Janet, when they were in a fight. She told everyone that Janet had been smoking cigarettes behind the school. But it wasn't true. I walk back there every day and I've never seen her, not even once.

I find my seat and without looking, I can tell exactly where Bobby is. All of a sudden, his whereabouts are important to me. What is he doing? Who is he talking to? Is he looking at me to see if I'm looking at him? Somehow, I make it through class without any eye contact from Bobby or disturbances from Sandra. The bell rings and I'm so ready to get home. I jump up and head for the door. That's when I hear it.

"Bye, Velvet."

Oh my Lord! Bobby Johnson said goodbye to me. "Bye, Bobby," I mumble back, reaching for the door handle as fast as I can. *Lord, please get me out of here.*

"See you Saturday," he adds.

I glance backward and see Sandra Shaw snap her head around. I'm sure she'll tell Janet within the next two minutes. I duck out the door, giving Bobby an "uh-huh" in response. I have no idea how to do this!

As Mercy and I walk home from school, neither of us stops talking. We interrupt each other and laugh at the craziness of the day. We're two teenagers with dates that aren't really dates on Saturday night. It doesn't seem real, but it sure feels good to be liked by Bobby. When Mercy and I part ways, I walk home with a smile I can't hide.

In the front yard, I stop at Mary's nubby feet. "I had a beautiful dream about your son," I tell her. "He was swinging with a little boy, and I think it was my brother. When you see them, tell them I say hi." I pause for a moment. "Oh, and a nice boy likes me. His name is Bobby."

I walk inside. Mama is putting out a cigarette, her feet are in slippers and dangling off the sofa. Why is she home so early?

"What's got you smiling so big?"

Oh no. I was hoping to keep this a secret. "Nothing. I guess just a good day. Home from work early?" I ask. Her glass of wine is on the table, between one sip left and almost gone.

"A good day, huh?" I can tell her curiosity is piqued. I walk to the kitchen and open a bag of chips, hoping the chewing will keep my smile contained. "What on earth happened? Did you find out a boy liked you or something?"

Oh my gosh! How does she know? I choke on a chip and cough until it falls out of my mouth in a soggy lump.

"Lordy!" Mama sits up straight. "I'm right! Aren't I?"

"Mama, it's no big deal. I found out Bobby Johnson has a crush on me is all."

"Little chubby Bobby? From across the street?"

"He isn't chubby anymore. Or little, for that matter. And he doesn't live across the street."

Mama sits back, ready to hear more. "You know what I mean! The chubby boy you used to play with."

"He's grown up over the years, a lot of the boys have." I don't mention his strong, broad shoulders or his piercing blue eyes or his thick, soft hair. What was once a tight buzz cut is now smooth, with long waves sweeping across his forehead. Thinking about his hair makes my stomach tingle. Is this what love feels like?

Mama comes into the kitchen and lights another cigarette. "How are you gonna respond?"

"Respond?"

"Hell, Velvet! He's gonna want to know if you like him too!"

I haven't even thought about that. It hasn't gotten further than me talking about him to Mercy. But Mama starts in with tried-and-true tips on how to win a man's heart. "I mean, a boy's heart," she corrects herself. "First, you dress like you like him. You know, a little extra effort. Maybe a sundress and some lip gloss and a good high ponytail. And stop wearing cardigans, for goodness' sakes. You look like Janet Evans and her clique of goody-goodies."

Come to think of it, Janet does pair all of her outfits with cardigans. Is that so bad? I pull at the edges of mine, suddenly uncomfortable. I reach up and touch my hair and feel the flyaway waves reaching for the ceiling. I palm them to push them down, but they pop back up the second I let go.

"Oh honey, it's gonna take more than your hand to calm those hairs. I've got just the thing!" Mama rummages in the cabinet under the bathroom sink. "Come here, Velvet! I'm gonna show you what it's like to get ready for a boy."

I'm not so sure I'm up for this right now, but Mama continues calling my name, determined to help.

"Mama, I'm tired."

"You can lay down after I fix you up right."

Mama sets out a towel and pulls out a small box I've seen under the sink for years. She motions for me to sit on the toilet while she takes everything out of the box. Using a brush, she rakes something dark and syrupy through my hair. "This may sting a bit," she says.

I nod like I understand, but I have no idea what she means by "sting" until the smelly liquid hits my head, and my nostrils burn from the smell.

"Ouch!" I squeal like a baby.

"It won't be much longer." She slops the liquid on quickly, and steps out of the bathroom.

"Where are you going?"

"To the kitchen. I'll be right back. I need some plastic wrap."

"Plastic wrap?" The burning sensation is causing me to sweat, and I fan myself with Mama's latest edition of Glamour magazine. I can't believe I'm letting her do this when I know she's been drinking.

"Well, shit fire, Velvet!" Mama yells from the kitchen. "We don't have any. I'm gonna have to run over to Mrs. Johnson's and borrow some."

She leaves me to burn alive on the toilet seat. I decide right here and now that Bobby Johnson is not worth this—no boy is. The door slams, and out the window I see Mama in her slippers, running past the overgrown garden and hollering, "Mrs. Johnson,

Mrs. Johnson!" I stand and look in the mirror to see if my head is in flames, but all I see is a goopy mess.

"Phew, just in time." Mama says when she returns, she pulls out a long sheet of clear plastic and wraps it around my head. "I hope I'm not too late."

"What do you mean, you hope?" To my horror, she pulls out the blow dryer, sets the temperature to high and points it at my head. "More heat? Mama, no! It's too hot as it is." I try to peek at my head in the mirror. How did I end up sitting on a toilet seat with my head on fire?

"Honey, it won't be but a minute. Hold tight now."

I take another look at the model on the magazine cover, then close my eyes and let the hot air burn through the plastic.

"Now, there." Mama turns the dryer off. "That wasn't so bad, was it?" As she peels the plastic away from my head, I wonder what "that" actually was.

Ditty lets herself in the front door. "Hello! Hello! Anybody home?"

"We're in here!" Mama calls to her.

Ditty sees me sitting on the toilet and says, "What in God's good name is going on in here?"

Mama steps back, beaming. "I gave Velvet a relaxer treatment to tone down her flyaway hairs."

And that's when I know something isn't right, 'cause Ditty gasps and puts her hand to her lips. "Lynette Marie Underwood, what on earth are you thinking?"

I start to cry. I don't even know why. I guess 'cause my scalp is throbbing, but also 'cause of Ditty's reaction to what she sees.

It must be bad. My tears fall faster than the faucet runs, right onto the magazine in my lap and the cover model's pretty face.

"Now, now," Mama says. "Stop crying, Velvet. It's not so bad. You haven't even seen it yet. Dry your tears and let me rinse it out over the tub."

I look down again at the magazine, and one of the stories jumps out at me, "Hairstyles You Need Now."

Mama runs cold water, which soothes my burning head. She rinses out the goop and shampoos and conditions my hair.

Ditty snaps, "I can't watch this a minute longer. I'm gonna go make dinner."

Mama dries my hair with a towel, and some of my hair falls out, right onto my lap. As I hold the fragile pieces that didn't make it through the fire, Mama starts whistling, which lets me know there's trouble. When her plans don't go right, she whistles to calm her nerves. And she's whistling up a storm now.

"How bad is it, Mama? Mama!"

Mama takes a step back. "I guess I should have gotten the plastic wrap before I started so I could have timed it better. But don't worry. It will be beautiful."

I gather strength and decide to have a look for myself. Mama moves to the doorway to make room for me in front of the sink. I think she wants a clear shot out of here, 'cause what happens next is enough to send Mrs. Johnson over to see if everyone is all right. I let out a full-fledged bloody murder scream. My hair lies flat against my head, and even though it's still wet, it looks as dry as the bales of hay lining the cornfields.

"Mama, what have you done?" I say over and over.

Ditty runs down the hall with Mrs. Johnson right behind her. Great! Now she'll tell Bobby how crazy Mama is and what a shame it is about my hair. All of us crowd into the tiny bathroom, staring at the disaster on my head. How am I ever going to go on a date that's not really a date now? I cry harder.

Mama nervously starts pulling conditioners out from under the sink. "Honey, it's OK, let's try this."

I squint my eyes and holler, "You aren't trying anything else on my hair! Ever!" I push everyone aside, even Mrs. Johnson, run to my room and bury my head under my pillow.

"Honey, you need a good conditioning treatment is all, and it will start to repair itself," Mama says from outside my door.

"Is that how this works? Broken things magically repair themselves?"

It's not surprising I end up back on the toilet seat, this time with Ditty spreading mayonnaise on my hair and wrapping my head with more plastic wrap. Mama stays in the living room away from me watching television. Ditty knows I don't want to talk. She smiles at me every time our eyes meet and keeps layering on the mayonnaise until my head is greasy and cool. I go back to earlier this morning when my hair wasn't burned to a crisp, and think about the journal and the baby, and break the silence.

"Ditty, did Mama ever have ... I mean ... want any other kids?"

Ditty lifts my chin up, and I can smell the eggy dressing on her hands. "What makes you ask?"

"She had me, but ..." I struggle to get the words out. "Did she always want me?"

Ditty's eyes soften. She tilts her head like she doesn't understand the question, then pulls me in close. "Of course she did. In fact, I was there the moment time stopped for a split second and your mama's soul and yours met for the very first time. I watched her eyes find yours and then she whispered something in your ear."

"What did she say?" I lean in closer.

"That's a secret between you and your mama and the sweet air that swirled around the room the day you were born. I'll tell you what, though." Ditty rubs my back with her dry hand.

"What?" I look up for the answer.

"She certainly wanted you."

The phone rings in the kitchen, and I hear Mama tell Mercy I'm not feeling well. Not feeling well is a major understatement. I march determinedly to the kitchen, Ditty close on my heels.

"Mama what are we gonna do about my hair? How are you going to fix it?"

Still holding the phone, she says, "Velvet, it'll be fine."

Ditty gives Mama a look that says otherwise, and I grab the phone out of Mama's hand. I don't want her to hear about the date, so I pull the phone cord as far as it will go—as far away from Mama as possible.

"The date that's not really a date is no longer happening," I whisper to Mercy.

"Why? What's going on?"

I don't bother to whisper anymore and let some slack out of the phone cord. "As a matter of fact, I don't think I'm gonna even bother going to school ... ever!" I want Mama to know she's ruined my life!

Mama gets up off the sofa, comes into the kitchen and says, "Young lady, pull yourself together. Us Underwoods don't let broken things beat us down."

Now I have her attention. I pull the receiver away from my mouth.

"Mama, are you kidding me? You've let a broken relationship beat you down so hard, you can't get up off the couch for a glass of water that's a foot away from you. So don't you talk to me about being beaten down. I've learned from the best."

Mama gasps as if a rabid raccoon has entered the house. She throws her head back and wails. Ditty comes down the hall from the bathroom, looks at me and says, "Lordy, Mrs. Johnson's gonna hear this and wonder what is going on over here. Lynette, why are you crying like that?"

"'Cause she's right," Mama sobs. "Velvet's right."

"Hello?" Mercy's voice comes through the receiver. "Everything OK?"

"Sorry, Mercy. We've had an incident over here. Mama decided to fix my hair, and now it's ruined. Completely ruined." I break into tears again and tell Mercy about the relaxer. "Apparently my waves were too unruly for Mama."

I think about all the times I've seen that box of fire in our bathroom and never knew it would ruin everything one day. I make a mental note to remove any and all suspicious packages from under the sink.

"Anyway, that's why I can't go to the movies with Bobby."

"Why don't you sleep on it, Velvet? I'll come by in the morning and help you with your hair. Don't lose hope."

"OK," I say, trying to sound positive.

Ditty is staying longer than usual, which I appreciate. Mama has found her way to her wine and is fighting sleep. Ditty takes the glass out of Mama's hand and tells her to go to bed. I sit in my room, my head still wrapped in mayonnaise, and listen to Ditty give Mama directions. I hear her help Mama get into her pajamas, tell her to go to the bathroom, and set a glass of water beside her bed. Finally she says, "Good night, Lynette. Tomorrow is another day."

Ditty stops in my doorway and says, "I hope you know your mama didn't mean any harm. She was trying to help."

I try to muster a nod like I understand, but I can't, 'cause I don't. "Do you think it will be better in the morning?" I ask.

"Honey, I think anything is possible. You sleep good now." She kisses my forehead and pats my plastic-wrapped head. "We'll worry about this tomorrow."

I'm not ready to go to sleep. My anger and frustration about Mama make me braver than usual. I walk into her bedroom, and without even bothering to look at her I head straight to the nightstand drawer. I take the journal, leaving the drawer open, walk back into my room and get comfortable on my bed. I find the page where I left off:

Dear Little One,

Just a few hours ago you were floating inside my belly. Now I'm looking at your tiny soul floating inside a glass. I never met you the way I should have, but somehow I miss you. I softened to the idea of you, and my heart held you like it had for a lifetime. You came so quickly, my heart didn't have time to process it. What I'm trying to say is, I didn't know I would love you until you were no longer here, and I'm so sorry. Now I'm left with an empty ache, a pain so deep the thought of you brings me to tears.

Your daddy didn't even know you were here, and he doesn't know you're gone. I wonder what he would have said about you. Would he have jumped up and down in excitement? Would he have stared in utter disbelief and fear? Or would he have grabbed me with his strong hands and held me tight, like his whole world was wrapped up in my 5-foot-6-inch frame? Truth is, I have no idea, and that's what scares me the most. He comes home tomorrow. I have to tell him about you. He needs to know.

I couldn't take you back to Dr. Dearberg's office and hand you over to his nurse so they could do God knows what with you. Then tonight, as I thought of the garden Pops and I built, I knew what to do. I found a shovel in the shed and dug. I looked over to where the moon reflected off the glass where you floated—you were so tiny. And while only a small hole was needed, I couldn't stop digging. With every shovel full of dirt, an agonizing sound, a mournful cry, escaped my body. I placed the glass where you floated in the hole, covering it with earth, covering my pain.

Pops and I planted yellow tulip bulbs last fall, and I got down on my knees and uncovered one perfect bulb. I placed the bulb into your final resting place and gently

*pushed it into the ground. Now every spring, when that
single tulip rises, I'll think of you in heaven and thank
God he put you inside me.*

I love you always,
Mama

Mama fell in love with the baby. My brother. She wasn't
sure about the baby because she was afraid of losing Diamond
Jim, but why was she so afraid? She didn't even know how he
would respond. And at what point do you care more about the
man hanging loosely off your arm than you do about the child
growing in your belly?

I can see it so clearly how Mama put Diamond Jim first in
everything. Even now, she puts the pain he caused ahead of
living her best life. She could have settled down with someone
else, married even.

Father Matthew says we shouldn't have false idols. I think
my daddy was a false idol to Mama, a love she thought she
needed to survive. I'll never do that. I'll never make someone so
important. If I can do that, I know I'll never end up like Mama.

I set Mama's journal down on my nightstand and look out my
window. The porch light is shining, and it outlines the garden. I
remember the lone yellow tulip. When I first noticed it years ago
I asked Pops, "How did all the tulips stay together except that
one?" He said he didn't know. Later he told Mama one of the
tulips had gotten away from the pack and said he'd move it back.

"No! Leave it." Mama snapped. Pops and I stopped what we

were doing and looked at her. "Please! I like it just the way it is."
Pops shrugged at me, and we let it be.

Now my eyes fixed on the spot where my brother is. I should
pray, but I don't know what to say. I pick up the journal again.
It's getting late. I scratch my forehead. I almost forgot it was
covered in mayonnaise and plastic wrap. I read a little more:

*Tonight DJ came back to Sack City. Instead of knocking
on the door, he sat in his car honking his horn. I was so
excited to see him, to hold him. If he'd known what I'd
been through the last couple of days, I'm sure he'd have
shown up with flowers, but how could he know what I
needed?*

*I ran out and reached inside his window to kiss him.
He pulled me through it, right onto his lap. The second he
touched me, my senses came back to life. He was home
and so was I. The sadness and the pain all disappeared.*

*He wanted to go for a drive and I agreed, even though
the front door of the house was still wide open. I glanced
at the door, knowing beyond that threshold was sadness
and loss, and I didn't want to remember it anymore. I
thought about telling DJ what Dr. Dearberg said about
his "rhythm method" not being reliable, but I stopped
myself. This was a fresh start. One little drive couldn't
hurt.*

*As he sped out of the driveway, I put my hand on
his thigh and leaned in to kiss his neck. His leg muscles
flexed and he sighed, letting me know he missed my
touch as much as I missed his. We drove past Ditty, who*

*was headed toward the house to check on me, and I
could hear her voice in my head, "Next time, you can get
pregnant the proper way." I pushed it away and we kept
driving, out of the trailer park, past the open field, into
the country. I felt so good to be by his side again.*

Just like that? The baby, my brother, means nothing? Why,
Mama? I don't understand. If Diamond Jim's happiness was
more important than a baby, then what do I mean? What was
it about him? I'm done with the journal. I don't want to read
anymore. I stomp back into Mama's room. I throw it in the
drawer of her nightstand and close it with a bang. She doesn't
move an inch.

I wake the next morning with plastic wrap stuck to the side
of my neck and remember it's Saturday. And oh yeah, Mama
ruined my hair, I have a date that's not really a date with Bobby
Johnson, and my baby brother is buried in the backyard.

CHAPTER 13

NOT REALLY A DATE

I head straight to the shower and watch the sloppy mess that's left of the mayonnaise flow down the drain. My hair does feel softer. Maybe Ditty was right. I dry off and wrap up in a towel. In the kitchen I find Mama is surprisingly up and at it, scrambling eggs and humming a happy tune like last night never happened.

"Velvet, it's gonna be beautiful today. I heard the weatherman say 70 degrees!"

Her cheerful take on the day makes me want to forget about last night, too. "That's nice." Which it is. I love spring weather. I open the front door to feel the fresh air and hear the birds chirping and fluttering around. I glance at Mary. The bud I planted by her toes looks bright and happy, and I'm overcome with guilt. Did I take my brother's flower from his grave? I run out to the garden in my bare feet. The ground is still cold.

Mama hollers, "Velvet, where are you going in just a towel?"

My eyes search the garden for clumps of bright green tulip buds—the bulbs she and Pops planted together—and for one lone bud. I can't find it and don't remember where it was. I first saw it so long ago, and the neglected garden has been covered in weeds for years now.

I open the rickety gate and continue to search the abandoned garden. Leaves are mashed together in wet piles and trapped along the fence in the corners. I have to find the tulip that marks my brother's grave, to know where he is buried. I walk to the far edge of the garden. Yes! This is where I saw it! I scoop the leaves away and throw them into a pile. I scoop and throw and scoop some more, until my freshly showered hands are covered in grime. As I move the last bit of soggy leaves away, I see it and fall to my knees. A little green bud rises up, free from the past that held it so tightly to the ground. I begin to cry, and I don't know exactly why.

Mama opens the kitchen window and shouts, "What on earth are you doing, Velvet Mary?"

"I … I …" What am I going to say? "Miss Fitzgerald told us to collect some dirt and bring it to school on Monday."

"Go get some dirt by the shed! Leave the garden dirt alone!" Mama is watching me, waiting for me to move.

I stare at the bud for a moment and whisper, "I see you."

"Let me get this straight," Mama says when I come back in the house. "You went flying out of the house—naked—to collect dirt without anything to put it in?"

"We're learning about what's in the soil. I wanted to check the dirt in the garden."

"The dirt in the garden is special, Velvet." Mama pauses and puts her hand on her heart. "I don't want you taking any of it out, not without asking me first. Now go wash your feet before you make an even bigger mess."

I shower again, washing away the dirt and the pain. Ditty stops by the house to check out her miracle hair cure, and she is quite pleased with the results. "We'll have to do another treatment on Sunday," she says. I have to say, my hair turned out nice and smooth, and Mama is walking around like a prize-winning beautician.

Mercy calls. She's delighted to hear about my hair and that our "date" is still on. We make a plan to walk into town casually and act like we're going to the movies. You know, a "nothing to see here, just two best friends going to a show" kind of night. I want to tell Mercy about Mama and my brother and the garden, and how she jumped right back into Diamond Jim's arms, but that will have to wait. I need to concentrate on the fact that I will see Bobby in just a few short hours.

"What are you gonna wear tonight?" Mercy asks me.

Because of my hair debacle and the journal, I haven't really thought about my outfit. I certainly don't want to ask Mama what to wear. God only knows what she'll try to push on me. Since the weather is getting nicer, I tell Mercy I'll wear something springy. "Maybe the chambray pedal pushers that Mama got me for my birthday last year, and a white T-shirt and Keds?"

I remember Mama waking me up on my 14th birthday. "Velvet, I've got some extra money to spend. How 'bout me and my special birthday girl go buy something nice?" We had so much fun together that day, doing normal mother-daughter things. The saleswoman let me wear my new pants right out of the store. Mama and I walked over to the diner and slurped on a big chocolate malt, piled high with whipped cream and a bright red cherry that Mama offered to me, even though they're her favorite. In one month, on May 1 to be exact, I'll turn sweet 16. I wonder if Mama has any surprises planned like last year.

"Sounds great," Mercy says. "What about your hair?"

I reach up to touch it again. "It's actually really soft and smooth." I say, surprised and not wanting Mama to hear.

"Do you still want me to come over and help you style it?"

"Yes, please!"

After we hang up, I look for my pedal pushers, which are folded neatly in my summer drawer. I pull them on and realize I've grown a few inches.

I find Mama in the kitchen. There's no one else to ask. "Do these still fit?"

Mama looks me over. "Hmm, let me see ... Stand back ... Bend down." I move in all kinds of positions and directions before she decides, "Yes, they sure do. But maybe we need to get you a new pair for your big birthday!"

Mama asks if I want anything to eat, but I'm so nervous about my date I say no. "I'm gonna lay down and read for a bit."

Mercy arrives right at 4 p.m., and I hear her talking to Mama in the living room.

"What are you girls up to this evening?" Mama asks Mercy.

"We were thinking about seeing a show." I don't think Mercy even knows what's playing at the theater. I yell for her to come to my bedroom. "Nice talking with you, Miss Underwood." She bounds into my room with a burst of energy. Her excitement is infectious. "Oh, Velvet! Your hair turned out fine! Let's put it in a high pony and tie a ribbon around it," she says as she strokes my locks.

"Sounds nice," I say as I look for some ribbon. "Mercy, isn't this crazy? The two of us getting ready for boys?"

We start to laugh, and suddenly Mama is standing in the doorway. "What's so funny, girls? You have a date tonight, don't you?" Mercy and I stand with our knees locked and our eyes wide. "I knew it!" Mama says, slapping her hand against her thigh. "That's why you got so upset about your hair, Velvet!"

"It's not a date, Mama." I lie. "We're getting ready for the movies."

"Uh-huh." Mama nods her head like she knows better. She comes all the way into my room and sits on the edge of the bed. "Girls, here's my advice ..."

"Mama! No!" I shout. *Please God, anything but words of wisdom from her about dating.*

"Velvet Mary! I do know a thing or two about boys." I turn toward the mirror above my dresser and let Mercy do the listening. "They may be quiet at first, and that's OK. In fact, they may not talk at all until you get into the dark theater. And that's when then they'll get their nerve up. About 25 minutes into the movie, they'll put their arm around your shoulder."

I look for Mercy's reaction in the mirror. She's listening to Mama intently, like she's in the first row at church and the pastor is speaking the God's honest truth.

"Be sure to put lotion on your arms. And wear perfume, of course."

I rub my arms to see if they're dry, and Mercy and I lock eyes in the mirror.

"Mama, OK. We get it." I can't control the sassy tone of my voice. Mama sighs and stands. I feel bad for rejecting her advice.

"Oh, and girls," she says, as she gets close to the door, "if they put a piece of chewing gum in their mouth, you can bet your sweet ass they're gonna try to kiss you."

Mama turns away with a grin and walks out the door. Once she's down the hall, I squeeze Mercy's arm and grab the body lotion and Mama's red bottle of perfume from the bathroom, and we get to work.

We make it to the center of town earlier than we wanted to. "I think our nerves are making us move faster," I say.

Mercy stops abruptly. "Take deep breaths," she says. "Inhale, exhale, inhale, exhale."

Once I've calmed down a little, I say, "Let's go."

The line to the theater is already filling with people. Tonight's feature is "The Trouble with Angels." We try not to look obvious as we search for Bobby and Tommy.

"Where are they?" I whisper to Mercy.

Mercy grabs my arm. "Right there. Don't look." Bobby is standing next to me in the popcorn line.

"Hi, Velvet," he says.

I manage a casual "Hi, Bobby." But when I turn around, my elbow hits the corner of the counter sending my popcorn flying out of the bucket and onto Bobby's loafers.

Bobby and I look at each other and laugh, just like we used to when we ran into each other playing night tag. "I'm so sorry," I say, holding the bucket tight to my chest.

"It's OK, Velvet. I usually spill popcorn everywhere too."

Mercy's talking to Tommy, her popcorn still safely inside her bucket. They make their way toward us, and she whispers in my ear, "Velvet, we're on our first date!"

We make our way to our seats and file in. Tommy goes in first, and Bobby pauses and waves Mercy past him like they have it all planned. Wait, I want to sit by Mercy! He pauses again and motions for me to sit. I smile at Mercy as I sit down and lean my body toward her armrest, away from Bobby. This is all too real. Too fast. Calm down, Velvet. Inhale, exhale, inhale, exhale. Am I doing it right? How's my hair? *Lord, I have no idea what I'm doing.*

The lights in the theater dim. My very first date has begun. Bobby Johnson is sitting next to me—on purpose—at the movies! He opens his licorice and asks if I want any. I shake my head no and mumble, "Thank you." Stop acting so weird, Velvet. I take another breath.

Bobby leans in closer to me. I keep my mouth full of popcorn and my straw close to my lips. A few times, Bobby leans forward to check on Tommy, like they have a plan they need to follow. Mercy and I smile at each other, and I remember what Mama said. Has it been 25 minutes yet? As I think it, Bobby yawns and stretches, and suddenly his arm is against the back of my neck. I go completely still. I want to look over at Mercy, but I can't. Oh, how I wish I'd worn a cardigan to cover my neck. The heat coming from Bobby combined with my nerves is too much.

The actors in the movie are funny, and the audience erupts in laughter, which helps diffuse the uncomfortable situation Bobby has created. He never moves his arm, not even a little. He's decided to put it there and there it will stay.

The Coca-Cola catches up to me. I have to pee, and I want Mercy to come with me. I try to turn my head, but with the weight of Bobby's arm bearing down on me, I can't. "Mercy ..." I mumble. "Mercy?"

"What is it?" She gets closer. Thank God she isn't trapped like I am.

"Bathroom?"

Mercy stands and asks if I'd like to join her in the ladies' room. Bobby finally releases his arm. The cool air on my neck is a welcome change as we get up to leave. I look back at Bobby before I turn toward the exit, and I see him huddling with Tommy.

"Well?" Mercy says.

"He did exactly what Mama said he would do!"

"Did you like it?"

Did I? "I honestly don't know. It felt uncomfortable and awkward. Did Tommy put his arm around you?"

"Yes, he did."

"And?" I ask.

"I kinda liked it," Mercy says.

We pee quickly and get back to our seats. Bobby takes a sip of his soda and unwraps something. And then I smell peppermint waft through the air and I'm terrified. I turn to Mercy and mouth, "Gum!"

Mercy shakes her head like she doesn't understand. I mouth it again. Then I pretend to chew gum. Her eyes widen. She looks at Tommy, and he's chewing gum too.

The movie soundtrack gets louder, and the scene intensifies. Then it happens. Bobby whispers, "Velvet?"

I turn toward him. "Yes?"

"Would it be all right if I kissed you?"

Bobby Johnson is going to kiss me. *Oh Lord Jesus, he's going to kiss me!*

I want to ask Mercy what she thinks, but I can't. I have to act fast. I decide it has to happen sometime—most girls my age have already had their first kiss. "I guess so," I say.

Bobby presses toward me, the smell of Doublemint gum hanging in the air between us, and his lips touch mine. It's so quick, I don't even think Mercy sees it. Afterward, he puts his arm back around me and takes a sip of his soda, like nothing even happened.

Lord, did it just happen? Did I do it right? What am I supposed to do now?

Bobby keeps his arm around me. His fingers are now confident enough to make contact with my bare skin. Thank goodness I put lotion on before I left. Thank you, Mama! I sneak a peek at Bobby—he looks happy about what just happened.

The movie ends and Bobby and Tommy say goodbye. Mercy and I walk arm in arm under the streetlights, eager to go over every little detail of our first date. Once we're far enough from the theater, I say, "Mercy, he kissed me. Bobby kissed me!"

Mercy's eyes widen. "Tommy kissed me too!"

I grab her and hug her tight, and we giggle about the details, which we'll remember forever.

"Mercy." I stop at a street sign before we cross. "The date that wasn't really a date turned into a real date!"

We both laugh.

"And, Velvet, your mama was right about that gum!"

We're laughing so hard we almost pee our pants.

"For once, Mama was right about something."

Mama is already asleep on the sofa when I get home, thank goodness. I don't bother to tell her to get up and go to bed. I turn off the television and the lights and head to my room. I could read Mama's journal if I wanted to, but all I want to think about is Bobby.

I untie the ribbon from my ponytail, place it in my own journal, and write at the top of the page:

Tonight, Bobby Johnson kissed me.

I close the journal with the ribbon dangling from the page and fall asleep imagining the weight of Bobby's arm around my shoulder.

CHAPTER 14
CHURCH

I dreamed about Bobby last night. We were at school, and I was having a really good hair day. I had on a pretty skirt that twirled every time I turned and a peach top that complemented my skin. I wore rose blossom-colored blush on my cheeks, and I was getting something unimportant out of my locker.

I heard someone running down the hall, and I turned on my heels to see Bobby coming out of the boys' locker room wearing his Sack High red tank top and gray gym shorts. He was carrying a white sweatshirt. His black Converse were untied, and his thick hair blew back as he raced down the hall. He must have been late for class because he was disheveled and rushing.

I smiled and waited for him to stop and say hi, but he ran right past me like I wasn't even there. He dropped his sweatshirt, and I called out his name, but it was too late. He was already around the corner and out of sight.

I looked around to see if anyone was looking and put the sweatshirt to my nose and inhaled deeply. That's when I discovered my new favorite scent: sweaty boy mixed with Tide.

"Velvet, are you up?" I hear Mama calling me, but I don't want to wake up from this dream. Why didn't Bobby stop and say hi? If I keep sleeping, maybe he'll turn around and kiss me. Just keep your eyes closed, Velvet. He'll come back. He didn't see you is all.

"Velvet?" Mama continues to holler. "I need my cigarettes. Would you mind getting them from the living room?"

I pull the covers up over my head and pray she'll stop yelling.

"Velvet!"

As quickly as Bobby turned the corner, the dream is gone. I can't get it back. I blink my eyes open reluctantly. I really want to scream, "Leave me alone!" But I don't. I twist out of bed until I'm solidly upright.

"I'm coming, Mama. Just a minute."

Mama is in the bathroom getting ready for something. I'm too tired to even ask what it is. I hand her the cigarettes.

"It's about time you woke up, Little Miss Sleeping Beauty. You better get ready, 'cause we're going to church today."

"Church?" It's Sunday, but why this Sunday? Mama is acting like she never misses church on a Sunday.

"Today is special and we're going."

I rub the sleep out of my eyes and wonder what exactly makes today so special.

"How was your date? I mean ... how was the movie with Mercy?" Mama points at the bottles of perfume and lotion Mercy and I left out.

"The movie was great," I say, avoiding eye contact at all costs.

"Uh-huh ... Tell me more." Mama takes a seat on the toilet and turns her knees to the side toward the round magnifying mirror propped up on the bathroom counter. She applies foundation to her cheeks and hums a soft song. When she's done, she searches for the perfect shade of blush. "Ah, Perfectly Peach!" she exclaims. She brushes on the pale powder and stands under the dim light above the big mirror to inspect her work. Her curls, softer than mine, frame her face loosely. "Well, go on."

"It was great. The date was great." There, I said it.

Mama pulls me in for a hug. "Oh, Velvet! Your first date!" She holds me like I've just won the Nobel Peace Prize and then pulls back and looks me straight in the eyes.

"Was there a kiss?"

Oh no. Does she need to know everything?

"A small one." Now the whole truth is out.

Mama smiles, claps her hands and turns around to hand me the same bottle of perfume Mercy and I used last night. "Here, sweetie. This is yours now."

I sniff the flowery fragrance and grin at her.

Mama makes up her eyes next. They're the color I imagine the ocean to be in the early morning, right before the sun and the moon pass each other, a soft blue-green. I've never seen the ocean, except for on TV and in movies. But it amazes me how God told the ocean to stop right there, like he drew a line on the beach so we could be safe and also enjoy it. Thinking about God and the ocean makes me eager to get to church. Besides, what if I happen to see Bobby there? I pull out my hairbrush and run it through my waves. I want to look good, too.

Mama spends about five minutes per eye—first a dark blue eyeliner on her top and bottom lids, followed by a few strokes of baby blue shadow. She pulls out a tube of black mascara, opens her lids real big and brushes it on, like a pastry chef applying the finishing touch of icing. After I brush my teeth, Mama hands me a tube of lipstick.

"You're gonna need this now."

"Mama, I don't want to wear lipstick. Not yet." What would the girls think at school if I showed up with bright red lips?

"Suit yourself." Mama pulls the top off, and her lips know it's coming, 'cause they instinctively make the appropriate O shape. Around in circles she goes, until she blows me a big red kiss in the mirror.

"You should get ready like this every day, Mama." I can't help but think what life would be like if every day was a church day.

We pull out of the driveway a few minutes later, and I glance at Mary. I have a feeling she knows where we're going and she's happy. Mama picks up Ditty, who slides reluctantly into the front seat of Mama's big white pickup truck, scooting me to the middle. I see the church marquee as we get closer: "If It Matters to You, Then It Matters to Him More!"

Mama parks in the first spot, closest to the door. She tells me to help Ditty get out—not an easy task 'cause the truck sits up so high. Meanwhile, Ditty's pulling her skirt down, staring at her reflection in the window, and playing with her hair until she's fluffed it just right.

"Hurry up, Velvet!" Mama shouts. "I don't want to sit at the back of the church with all the sinners."

Ditty mutters, "What in the hell is she talking about?" I keep Ditty moving and shake my head, praying God will forgive us: Mama, for thinking her sins are less than everyone else's;

Ditty, for saying the word hell on church property; and all of us combined, for not attending Mass on a regular basis.

The tall wooden doors at the front of the church are propped open, and Father Matthew is standing there greeting the congregation. His arms are outstretched, and he's dressed in a beautiful thick white robe with red and gold tassels draped around his neck. He reaches for Mama's hand, and before she grabs his, she whispers, "Velvet, stand up straight and pull your shoulders back."

"What have we here?" Father Matthew beams at us. "The good Lord has certainly blessed us today."

Mama squeezes his hand with both of hers. "Good morning!"

Father Matthew stares straight into Mama's eyes. "God bless you, Lynette. I've been praying for you. And oh, Velvet! What a beauty you've grown into."

I can't help but notice Mama seems starstruck by Father Matthew. She even curtsies before she sashays into the church.

Ditty is already standing at the front pew, ready for Mama to hurry up and stop acting like a fool in front of Father Matthew. I walk behind Mama, and I'm so proud to be here. I'm also happy we're among the first to arrive, 'cause if the congregation saw Mama with Father Matthew, acting like a teenage girl who just met Elvis for the first time, they might just believe the rumor that Lynette Underwood lost her mind the day Diamond Jim left her. I look around every few minutes for Bobby and his family, but I don't see him. I can't tell if I'm relieved or disappointed.

Mama kneels before she enters the pew and prays while she waits for the service to begin. I've never seen her pray like this.

The music starts and everyone—except Ditty, who has fallen

asleep beside me—grabs a big green hymnal book and turns to the song "Leave Your Trouble at the Water." The choir sings sweetly, and Mama hums along. I'm wrapped up in the music, wondering if everyone else feels the way I do. Father Matthew taught us once that the Holy Spirit doesn't ask permission to enter our hearts, he just does. And sometimes he does it through song.

I nudge Ditty 'cause I don't want her to miss the Holy Spirit. But she blinks and goes back to sleep. The choir sings, "Turn your back on your trouble, walk down to the water, and let your sorrow drown in God's loving embrace. Oh yes, leave your trouble at the water."

I look up at Mama and watch tears flow over the foundation she applied earlier. She closes her eyes and continues to hum and sing. "Oh yes, leave your trouble at the water. Set it down. Set it down and soar with God."

Father Matthew begins the service with "Good morning," and when the people of Sack City say it back to him, he smiles like we've all done a good job saying hello. Then he asks, "Have you ever wondered if God is listening?" Father moves his eyes around the room to see everyone's reaction. "I mean, really listening?" Some people nod their heads, while others look off into the distance. My eyes move up to the cross where Jesus is. Father Matthew continues. "You know the days when the wind is blowing?" He pauses again. "You may feel it on your cheeks, and it may mess your hair … unless you're Mr. Willoughby." Everyone chuckles, especially Mr. Willoughby, who's sitting in the front row rubbing his bald head. "But you know what I mean." Father draws us back in. "You can feel the wind. You don't have to ask if it's blowing because you know it is. Well, God is like the wind, always there, but sometimes you go outside and there's no breeze at all. Nothing. No trees rustling, no flowers waving ..." Father walks closer to the pews, closer to the people of Sack City. "And it's in these moments we wonder where God has gone."

I look over at Mama who's nodding in agreement. "My friends, when you can't feel the wind, when you think you can't find God, call to mind the people who surround you. Can you find God in them? Maybe it was the phone call checking in, the nudge you needed to keep your chin up, the touch of a hand on your back for support. God is always at work. The wind is still there, even if you can't feel it blowing."

Mama reaches for my hand and Ditty's, which wakes Ditty from her nap. I squeeze Mama's hand tightly. "In Jeremiah 29, the Lord says, 'I will listen to you.'" Father pauses again. "But do you know what he says next?" He looks around the room, like he's waiting for a response. "He says, 'I will listen to you if you seek me and find me, and when you seek me with your whole heart.'" The energy in the church feels different. Bowed heads look up and shoulders roll back. Everyone is at attention as Father Matthew lets scripture linger in the air. "Brothers and sisters, I ask this simple question: Are you seeking God with your whole heart?"

I sit back in the pew and pull my dress down toward my knees. Am I?

"God is listening, I promise. You are on his mind, and he loves you. Seek him like an orphan yearns for a father, and with an open heart, ready to be moved by the gentle winds of the Holy Spirit."

Father motions to the organist to play as he prepares the altar for Holy Communion. We all pick up our hymnals again. Mama sings, "Cause your word to come alive in me; Give me faith for what I cannot see; Holy Spirit, breathe new life in me."

Instead of singing, I pray: *Lord, I know you are at work. I feel you. Bring new life to Mama, breathe into her the power of the wind, the power that moves the dead leaves off the trees and blows them far, far away.*

After the service is over, Mama goes over to the row of red candles lined up under the Virgin Mary and lights only one.

Father Matthew waits at the doors and says to us, "I do hope you all come back again soon."

Ditty scurries off ahead of us toward the car. She's done with Mass. But Mama nods, this time more poised. "We certainly will, Father."

All the way home, Ditty talks about what she's making for lunch. "I'm gonna slice leftover pork, fry some onions, and put them on toasted bread with mayonnaise." My mouth starts watering.

When she's done discussing lunch, Ditty asks, "What was that nice preacher man saying this morning?"

I look at Mama expecting a laugh, but she doesn't say anything. She's driving with her window down, deep in thought as the wind blows gently against her forearm.

CHAPTER 15
PIE

I go to bed Sunday night with a funny feeling in my stomach about Monday. Will it be weird between me and Bobby? Especially after the kiss?

God, thank you for today, for church, for Mama and Ditty. I have a favor to ask, though: Can you make tomorrow not awkward? I know it will be just as it is, but maybe you could help make me not so awkward? Amen.

I awaken with an eagerness to get ready for school, but not my normal kind of ready. I take Mama's advice and rub my body with lotion and spray on some of the perfume she gave me. I even dab on a little red lipstick.

When I see Mercy waiting at our tree, she says, "Velvet, I can smell you coming from here!"

"I used the perfume again."

"Yes, I can tell."

When Mercy laughs, I panic and cover my red lips. "Is it too much?"

"Nothing that the wind and fresh air can't blow off. Your

lips look goood." Mercy's grin is as wide as Main Street running through Sack City is long.

I smile at the notion of the wind fixing things that aren't quite right. "I'm nervous to see Bobby. Are you nervous to see Tommy?"

"A little, but just act normal, Velvet."

"Normal. OK," I say, without any confidence at all.

"Don't forget," she says, "we're going to get pie after school!"

Mercy and I love to collect glass bottles and take them to the grocery store for spare change, and we've finally gotten together enough coins to buy one piece of blueberry pie at Bigsby's. Even if Mrs. Evans owns the shop, her pie makes her musings about Mama almost bearable.

By the time we get to school, the orange juice I drank for breakfast is sloshing around in my stomach. Mercy and I see Janet and Sandra standing at their lockers whispering to each other. When they notice us, they huddle closer and whisper some more.

"They're talking about us," I say.

"I know," Mercy says.

"Do you think they know about the date?" I ask. Mercy nods yes. "How would they know?" I whisper.

"Tommy is Janet's neighbor. I bet he told her."

We both try not to scan the halls for Bobby and Tommy, but somehow, we do. So far, no sightings. Mercy and I part ways. "I'll see you at lunch," I say. "Good luck." I look up at the clock. Only two periods until I see Bobby.

Classes go by quickly and my stomach doesn't stop gurgling

one bit. I have everything I need, but I feel like wasting time and go to my locker anyway. When I get there, Janet Evans sidles up next to me. "Nice lipstick, Velvet. I heard about your date."

"It wasn't really a date." I snap back.

"I heard he kissed you. Just so you know, he kissed me first." Janet has a smug look on her face. How does she know about the kiss?

"OK." I don't know what else to say, so I look around for Mercy. She probably went straight to her next class. I see Bobby turn the corner and pause when he sees Janet talking to me.

"Bobby told Sandra he still likes me. You should know that."

"OK," I say again. Why can't I think of anything to say? I grab something I don't need out of my locker and close the door. Janet doesn't move, so I step to the side and walk away. *Lord, remember when I asked you to help make me less awkward? Were you listening?*

I go to class and take my seat. Bobby walks up behind me and puts a note on my desk. I have no words. It's like my voice is trapped behind a big steel door. I grab the piece of paper and put it inside my book. Class starts and I spend the hour pretending to pay close attention to what my teacher is saying, but all I can think about is the folded square of paper wedged in the middle of my history book and whether Bobby liked kissing me more than Janet. I crack open my book and make sure the note is still there and that I didn't imagine it. As the bell is about to ring, I look back at Bobby, who is gathering his things. I make a beeline to lunch to find Mercy.

"Mercy, Bobby wrote me a note. And Janet knows about the kiss … she said Bobby kissed her first!"

"What? How? What did the note say?"

"I haven't read it yet."

"Follow me." Mercy leads me straight to the girls' bathroom. I pull out the note.

Dear Velvet,

Thank you for joining me at the movies the other night. I wanted to say you smelled really good, and I hope I didn't scare you off with the kiss. Anyways, I really like you.

Sincerely,
Bobby

PS: Please write back.

Mercy and I jump up and down. "Velvet! What a sweet note!"

I can't stop smiling.

On our way to lunch, we pass Bobby and Tommy at their table. Mercy says, "Hi, Tommy," and I smile at Bobby, unable to muster up the same confidence as Mercy. While she and I eat, Janet and Sandra give us mean looks the entire time.

"I'm going to write Bobby back before Mrs. Holden's class."

"Good idea. What will you say?"

I pull out my notebook and write.

Dear Bobby,
Thank you. You smelled good too, and I liked your shoes.

Sorry about spilling popcorn on them! The kiss was nice.
I like you too.

Sincerely,
Velvet

"It's perfect!" Mercy says. I smile at her and fold the note.

Mercy and I see each other in the hall again before last period. "I forgot to tell you I saw Tommy talking to Janet earlier this morning," she says. "They're just friends. I bet she asked him about our date. Ignore her. She's up to no good. Are you ready to give Bobby your note?"

"Yes." As I walk into class, I go right up to Bobby and put the note on his desk. Janet and Sandra are in class too, and they watch the whole exchange.

Again, my mind is preoccupied, and I have no idea what we're learning. Thank goodness Miss Fitzgerald doesn't ask me any questions. But then she says, "Class, I'd like for you to pick a partner for your science project."

I hate partner projects. I look back at Bobby. Janet is already at his desk, and I see him nod yes. Willard McClukin, Jr., the mayor's son, leans over and asks if we can be partners. Oh no, not Willard. "Sure," I say.

I don't talk to Bobby after class. I guess I'm a little jealous he said yes to pairing up with Janet so quickly. I wonder if he was trying to get to me. If he was, it worked, 'cause I don't like the way it feels. No, it's Janet's fault. I won't let her get to me. Bobby was just being polite. I picture Mama watching Diamond Jim and Mrs. Evans cozied up at the bar.

At Bigsby's, Mercy and I sit at the counter and decide we're tired of talking about boys. We move on to pie instead. It doesn't take Mrs. Evans long before she starts asking about Mama.

"Velvet … How is your mama doing?" She leans in, her catty tone smothered in sugary sweet charm. I feel the urge to pull away from her, to avoid her and her words altogether. "She used to live a real exciting life, back when she was dancing at the Hip Joint."

I've never minded hearing stories about Mama's dancing. To me, they reveal a strong, confident woman, and I love to imagine Mama like that.

"We'd like a slice of blueberry pie, please," Mercy says before I can respond.

Mrs. Evans pulls out a whole pie from the revolving glass case and cuts a wedge for us. Just then, Janet and Sandra walk in and sit in a booth. "Ignore them." Mercy whispers.

"Mrs. Evans, that's so nice of you to remember my mama like that. She is real, real proud of her dancing days and how she was the featured performer five days a week. Everyone just loved her routines."

Mrs. Evans crinkles her nose and slides our piece of pie onto a plate and across the counter. "You girls enjoy, now."

"Velvet, was your mama really the featured dancer?" Mercy asks.

"Yes, she was. Men would line up around the corner to see her dance." Mrs. Evans tries to look busy but it's obvious she is listening intently. "Quite a few men proposed to her—and one time she almost said yes!"

I try to imagine Mama married, but I can't. Since DJ left, her heart hasn't been at home in her own skin. I keep talking, a little louder now, so Mrs. Evans can hear me. "When some people think about exotic dancers, they think about girls who've gotten themselves into trouble and don't have a good home." Mercy nods. "But that wasn't the case with Mama at all. Ditty always said, 'It wasn't like that then, Velvet. It was good clean fun. Nothing raunchy going on in back alleys. Church men, Godly men, just looking to watch a beautiful woman dance and have a nice time.'"

Mrs. Evans can't help herself. "Dancing for married men ain't exactly 'clean fun,'" she says.

I don't know what to say, so I dig into my pie before Mercy eats it all. Mrs. Evans has new customers, which takes the attention off us. She stops back as I'm taking my last bite. "Oh, Velvet dear, please do tell your Mama our old friend DJ is in town. I'm sure she'd love to know."

I choke on a blueberry. Mercy slaps my back as we watch Mrs. Evans nonchalantly walk to the other end of the counter. We leave and Mercy hugs me in the parking lot. "It's gonna be OK."

"Do you think it's true, Mercy? Do you think he's really here?"

My eyes scan the streets for him. I wonder if he's watching me right now.

Mercy and I walk home in silence. We part ways at our tree, and I wonder what state Mama will be in when I get home. She's already in her pajamas, feet propped up, hair in curlers. I mention all the things Mrs. Evans said at Bigsby's and watch Mama's mouth contort like she's about to spit out something disgusting. "And ..." I hesitate. "She said to tell you DJ is in town."

Mama pulls her spine straighter than a two-by-four.

"That jealous hussy can shove another piece of liar's pie in that big ol' mouth of hers. Who the hell does she think she is?" She mumbles as she gets off the couch, "C'mon, Velvet."

"Where are we going?"

"We're going to Bigsby's."

My stomach drops. "Mama, you're in your pajamas, and your hair is in curlers."

Mama pauses at the front door. She turns and walks down the hall to the bathroom, and I hear curlers drop one by one into the sink. She pulls a blue sweater over her silk pajama top, slips on a pair of blue jeans and grabs the first pair of high heels she sees. She rakes her hands through her wavy hair. She looks beautiful without even trying.

"Now let's go get some pie!" Mama holds the door open for me, and I reluctantly walk through. I guess part of me wants a little revenge too. *Forgive me, Lord.*

Outside, Mama inhales the cool air and walks to the truck. Her high heels don't even stumble on the gravel driveway.

"You sure do walk good in those shoes." I say, trying to distract her.

"Sugar, you know I know how to get around in heels. I'm gonna march these heels right up to that pie-peddling bitch and give her a piece of my mind."

Lord, I know she doesn't mean to call Mrs. Evans the B word. She's angry is all.

"Mama, do you think that's wise? Let's think about this for a second." I can't look at her. I gaze down at my feet. The more I think about it, I really don't want to be a part of this. Will I ever be able to eat at Bigsby's again?

"Velvet, sometimes a woman has to stand up for herself, and this is one of those times." She puts the truck in reverse and then pauses. "Shit fire."

I turn my gaze toward the sky. *Sorry, Lord.* "What is it?" I ask.

"Truck's on empty. We need gas." Mama reaches for her purse, which is shoved behind her seat, and fumbles through her wallet. "We have exactly $12."

Mama puts the truck in drive and heads down the road to Sullivan's Auto Body, which is about a mile away. When Mr. Sullivan sees us pull up, he walks out to greet us. Mama rolls down the window, and he smiles at her tenderly. "What do we have here?" he asks.

"Just two good-looking gals and a truck that needs gas." Mama winks at me and pulls her hair over her shoulder. I can tell she's trying to look pretty. But why? She never gave Mr. Sullivan a chance after Diamond Jim left.

"I'm gonna have to agree," he says, still smiling. "Hi there, Velvet!"

I smile back and give a small wave. "Hi."

"Lynette, how many miles you got on this truck?" Mr. Sullivan asks.

"Too many," she says.

He nods and straightens his cap, "Sometimes the ones that are worn well are the ones worth keeping."

Mama grins. I think she's blushing. Does he think Mama has worn well? I don't want to know.

"Mr. Sullivan, could you please fill this worn-out old truck with $12 worth of gas?" Mama asks.

"You bet. Let's get you two beauties back on the road." Mr. Sullivan whistles as he fills up the tank. Mama watches the numbers on the pump circle around like a slot machine … $11.12 … $11.50 … Mr. Sullivan shifts back and forth in the brown work boots he's stood in for years. He examines his hands, which are stained with motor oil. I notice his face is sweet, handsome and rugged.

I whisper to Mama, "He's kinda handsome, don't ya think?" Mama shushes me and keeps her eyes pinned to the gas pump. She can't hide her smile. I can't help but think Mr. Sullivan must smell like gasoline and fresh air. When the numbers hit $11.98, he gently squeezes the handle on the nozzle until the pump says $12 exactly. Mama sighs in relief as Mr. Sullivan screws the gas cap back on and gives the cover a good, hard push. He wipes his hands on his coveralls as he walks back to Mama's window.

"Twelve dollars on the dot."

Mama smooths out the crumpled bills and hands them over. Their hands touch and they both flinch. Mama's cheeks flush even more.

"Have yourself a good evening, Mr. Sullivan," she says.

"You too, Miss Underwood."

Mr. Sullivan tips his cap and makes way for us to drive out.

With no other customers to wait on, he watches us take a right and head straight toward the center of town. I hope Mama's interaction with him might cool her off, but we head to Bigsby's with enough gas to get us there, and enough fight in Mama to set Mrs. Evans straight.

We pull in just before 5 p.m., and I see Mrs. Evans through the window, boxing up a pie. Janet is doing her homework in the same booth she was in when I left. Sandra must have gone home. Mrs. Evans looks up as we pull in, and I can read her lips as she says, "Holy shit."

Mama tugs at her sweater to make sure her pajama top isn't showing and heads for the door. She turns to look at me.

"Are you coming or what?"

Truth is, I want to stay right here in the truck, away from any drama. It's better not to witness some things. But Mama stands firm in her stance, insistent that I am by her side, so I reluctantly slide out of the truck and join her.

The bells on Bigsby's front door jingle as we enter.

"Well, well, well. Look what the cat dragged in," Mrs. Evans says.

Mama walks briskly up to the counter.

"Let's cut the crap, shall we?" She glares at Mrs. Evans. "You don't know me. You only know what your jealous, lying, back-stabbing, hungry heart has fed you. And from the looks of your ass, you've spent a whole lotta nights eating a whole heap of lies."

Mrs. Evans' jaw drops so low I wonder if it might hit the counter.

"So why don't you keep your bullshit comments about me, my past, and my daughter to yourself. Better yet, shove them up your sorry ass."

Mama jabs her finger in Mrs. Evans' face.

"And for the record, there is nothing—not one damn thing—you could tell Velvet that she doesn't already know. Are we clear?"

"Does she know her daddy, Diamond Jim, is in town? Or did you forget to tell her who her daddy is?"

Mama locks eyes with Mrs. Evans, flips open the lid on the white box, and digs her hand into the pecan pie inside it. Mrs. Evans gasps, and my eyes widen. I'm afraid of what's about to happen next.

Mama slowly brings her fingers to her mouth and licks them. Then she turns to face Janet, who's trying to hide behind her book, and says, "Janet, don't be like your mama, who has nothing better to do than fill her face with liar's pie. Unless you want to end up with an ass like hers."

"Get out of my shop!" Mrs. Evans hollers. "Everything everyone says about you is true! You just done and confirmed it! Diamond Jim was justified in leaving you. You ain't nothing but a crazy, drunk, used-up woman."

My heart thumps fast and hard. Mama stands calmly, slowly shaking her head. She waves her hand dismissively in the air.

"Crazy, no. Drunk, sometimes. Used up? Hell, no!"

Mama turns toward the door, grabs my hand and pulls me with her. It's a good thing she's dragging me because I feel paralyzed. An hour or so ago I was enjoying a piece of pie at this very counter, and now I'll probably never be allowed back.

"Let's go, Velvet," Mama says. "There ain't nothing here worth fighting for."

Once we're in the truck, I realize I'm shaking.

"Mama, what was that all about?" I ask.

She peels out of the parking lot, her breath matching her speed—fast and furious.

"Please slow down and tell me what that was all about."

She keeps driving.

"Mama!" I shout.

I pray no one is watching us as she finally pulls over on Ripple Street in front of Cleaver's Pharmacy.

"Velvet," she says calmly, "some women are born jealous. Joan Evans has a spiteful heart, and it was about time I put her in her place. She has always wanted your daddy, and she never got over the fact he chose me, and we had a family."

Mama continues, "When your daddy left, no one cheered louder than her. She was happy to see me hurt. Some people get a thrill when they see other people down."

"Do you think he's really here? In Sack City?" I ask.

Mama looks down at the steering wheel.

"Sugar, I don't know. He'll come find us if he wants to." She turns to look at me. "And I'll be ready for him."

I don't know what she means by that, and I don't ask.

"How did I look in there, Velvet?"

"You looked angry," I pause. "And strong. And beautiful."

"Good."

Mama puts her sticky pie hand on my thigh and squeezes it. She turns on her blinker and pulls back onto the street like nothing happened. I know it won't be long before the whole town hears about the cat fight at the pie counter.

CHAPTER 16
RED RIBBON

Once my heart has stopped racing, I feel proud of Mama. Seeing her stand up for herself makes me wanna stay up and talk with her long after we leave Bigsby's. Instead of her usual wine, she swirls a big glass of ice water.

"Velvet, did you see the look on her face?"

Poor Mrs. Evans didn't see it coming. One minute she was serving up blueberry pie, and the next she was being served a big ol' slice of humble pie by none other than Lynette Underwood.

"I think she got the message, Mama."

Mama nods and sips her water, her bare feet propped up on the coffee table. "It was about damn time," she says. "And it felt good too!"

Mama and I giggle, remembering Mrs. Evans' reaction.

"Velvet, you know your birthday is in a few days … I can't believe you're going to be 16 years old. Sixteen!" Mama beams at me. "It feels like only yesterday you came, and it was you and me against the world."

I smile at her, curious if she sees Diamond Jim in the image when she looks back that far.

"You and me and my daddy, right?"

I don't like how the word daddy feels leaving my lips, and I wish I could pull it back in.

Mama shifts uncomfortably in her seat like something is poking her bottom. "He didn't stay long enough to deserve an honorable mention."

Mama's right, and since the subject has come up, it seems like the right time to ask. I swallow hard to keep my nerves down. Here goes nothing.

"Hey Mama, do you ever think about finding Diamond Jim?"

I watch her closely to see if my question sets her back. There's a long pause.

"Sometimes ... I guess."

Sometimes? Yes!

"Well, I was thinking maybe we could ... you know ... try to find him ... together."

Mama goes completely still, like my question sucked all the energy right out of her body and the room. I try to get it back, to get her back.

"I just think if I could meet him, I could show him what a fine job you did raising me."

Mama starts drawing on the outside of her water glass. I watch as her finger moves in circles. Oh no. I've lost her.

She gets up from the couch.

"I guess I better be getting to bed. That pie fight really tired me out."

She stops to pat my head before she walks back to her bedroom. I'm left sitting alone, wondering if I've ruined my chances of finding Diamond Jim.

I put Mama's water glass in the kitchen sink and shut off the lights. I attempt to shut off the porch light, even though I know it'll be on until the darn bulb burns out again.

I whisper, "Did you see what happened at Bigsby's today, Pops? Mama still has some fight left in her. I bet you were proud." I smile up at the sky, searching for Pops, for answers. And though I wish Mama had answered my question, I'm still smiling when I lay my head on my pillow and pray:

Dear God, tonight I watched Mama come to life. Even though it may not have been holy, it was a glimmer of hope and an answered prayer. Did you see her drinking a glass of water? A miracle! So I want to say thank you. I know tomorrow Janet will be mad as a hornet, and I pray I can have the quiet confidence to defend Mama without causing a big fuss. I probably should be more worried about what Janet will tell Bobby, but I'm not nervous about that at all 'cause I know you'll be right by my side. I pray Mama is thinking about what we talked about tonight, finding my daddy, and maybe you could give her some more courage and fight? I'd really appreciate it. Amen.

The following day, Mercy came knocking on my door early.

"Am I running late?"

"No! I heard about the fight at Bigsby's."

So everyone already knows, and Mercy wants all the details. Mama has left for work early (another miracle!), and Mercy follows me to the bathroom so I can finish getting ready.

"What happened?" Mercy closes the toilet seat and sits on it.

"I told Mama what Mrs. Evans said to us after school, and she finally decided to give her a piece of her mind. It was really something. At first, I was embarrassed about how she acted, but now I'm proud. Really proud."

"Do you think Janet will say something about it at school?"

"I'm trying not to think about it."

I reach for the perfume, spray it on my wrists and rub them together like Mama taught me. Mercy asks if she can have some, too, and I hand her the bottle. All because of one little date, lotion and perfume are now part of my daily routine. I open up the top drawer and find Mama's lipstick.

"You putting on lipstick too, Velvet?"

I nod yes. I guess turning 16 is changing me more than I would have thought. Ditty always asks on my birthday, "Do you feel older, Velvet?" and usually, I say no. But something feels different—like puttin'-on-perfume-and-lipstick different.

"What did you hear, anyway?" I ask Mercy.

I pucker my lips like Mama does.

"My auntie called my mama on the phone and told her that Miss Underwood walked into the pie shop and gave Mrs. Evans a piece of her mind."

I put the top back on the tube and admire the sheen on my lips.

"You know, Mercy, I think Mama's been carrying around too much of the past for too long, and it was time to let some of it go." I picture Mama walking with a spring in her step now 'cause the weight of the world is gone. "I'm sure Janet will be in rare form today."

Mercy nods. She looks toward Mama's room.

"Have you read any more of the journal?"

"No, but I've been thinking about it."

"We have a few minutes now. Should we look?"

I scan the house making sure no one is home.

"OK, real quick."

We go to Mama's room and open the drawer, but the journal isn't there. I rummage through the drawer.

"Mercy, it's not here. It's gone."

Mercy looks around and sits on the bed. She looks under Mama's pillow. Nothing there. She picks up the pillow next to it—there it is. Mercy hands me the journal, and I find where I left off and read out loud to her:

I haven't written in a while, not since I lost the baby. I never got up the nerve to tell DJ, the timing never felt right. Dr. Dearberg gave me a pamphlet about diaphragms and said we should use condoms in the meantime. I brought it up to DJ, said if we aren't more careful, we could get pregnant. He just laughed and hugged me and said, "There's nothing to worry about—my method always works." I could have told him then—should have told him—but I was put off by his attitude. How could he be so sure? What made him think he was so perfect?

"I feel dirty reading this, Mercy," I say, looking away from the page.

Mercy nods in agreement. "Maybe skip a little bit," she says.

I look at the clock. We have 10 minutes before we need to leave. I scan the pages for some good news, something that won't leave me feeling like I need to go to confession. And then I see it:

I'm pregnant. AGAIN!

Mercy and I squeal.

"This is me!" I hold the journal like it's a gift I've always wanted and just received. "She's pregnant with me!"

I read eagerly:

I had all the same symptoms I did before. This time I made an appointment with the doctor and came back for the results a couple of weeks later. I was so happy when Dr. Dearberg announced, "I hope this is the news you were hoping for, Lynette ... you're going to be a mother!" A mother! This time, everything feels different. I'm not as scared, and Dr. Dearberg has been so nice about it. He said that it's not uncommon for women to miscarry again, and that I need to take it easy. He suggested I cut back on dancing for a bit. Give the baby some time to settle in. So that's what I'm doing. DJ hasn't asked about it; he's mainly interested in himself. He does seem a bit irritated that I'm not always giving him everything he wants when he wants it. Thankfully, bowling league playoffs are right around the corner, and he's been keeping busy practicing with his team. I'm grateful for it, 'cause it keeps him from trying to undo my pants at any given moment. I do miss his touch, but the nausea leaves me completely uninterested.

I don't exactly love him being at the Strike Zone so much without me there, 'cause Joan Evans plays in the league. She's still up to no good, but I'm not as worried now that I'm carrying his child. But like I said, bowling is keeping him occupied. Heck, who knows, maybe this baby will prompt him to put a ring on my finger and make me his forever girl! I can't help but imagine what it'd be like to call DJ my husband.

I don't want to stop reading, but Mercy interrupts, "We're gonna be late for school if we don't leave now."

I reluctantly put the journal back in the drawer.

"Velvet, remember?" Mercy says. "Under the pillow."

I put it back where we found it and notice something else. Another journal? She's as surprised as me when I pull out a stack of cards with a red ribbon tied around them. I look at Mercy like we've struck gold.

"What are those?" Mercy tries to reach for them, but I pull them closer.

"Birthday cards."

I untie the red ribbon with shaky hands, and it falls on the floor. The cards fall on Mama's unmade bed.

"Read one, Velvet."

I pick up a card. The front of it reads, "Happy Birthday to My Darling Daughter." I look at Mercy. She gasps and draws her hands to her mouth. I shake my head no. I open it and see a handwritten signature inside:

With all my love, Daddy

CHAPTER 17
BOOBY BLONDE

The clock on Mama's bedside table ticks loudly. Mercy reaches for the cards. I stand motionless.

"This is a good thing, right Velvet?"

I don't know what to say back. Mercy picks up the ribbon from the floor. She quickly places the cards back in a stack. I stare at them. We don't count them, but there have to be at least a dozen. I imagine my daddy standing at the five-and-dime, carefully choosing each card just for me. I feel like I do when I stare at his face at the Strike Zone—stuck in a moment, wondering why.

"He wrote to you. On your birthday. Every year!" Mercy reaches for my arm, and I cry because I have to.

"Why did Mama hide these from me?"

Mercy tucks the cards beneath Mama's pillow like that's where they belong.

I shout through my tears, "Leave them out! I want her to know I saw them."

Mercy looks back at me. "Are you sure you want to do that?"

I don't know what I want. Nothing makes sense. I wipe my tears and smudge the red lipstick across my cheek.

"It's gonna be OK, Velvet. I promise," she says and pulls me towards the bathroom. She dabs at my tears and wipes the red stain off my cheeks. She lays the stained towel neatly folded on the counter.

"It's time for school."

God bless Mercy for letting me walk in silence. Once in a while, she reaches over and rubs my back. We pass the drugstore. There are Mother's Day banners in the window, and I notice all the birthday cards and party decorations.

"Maybe he bought them here?" I ask Mercy. "Do you think he's been here the whole time?"

Mercy doesn't respond, and I don't blame her. Only Mama knows the answers, and I'm sure as heck gonna find out what they are.

We approach the school and see Janet near the entrance. I forgot all about the pie shop fight until this very moment. *Lord, have mercy on me today. Please. I don't know what I'll do or say.*

"I know what will cheer you up! Let's plan a second date for your birthday!"

"That'd be nice." I smile because Mercy is such a great friend.

"I'll make sure Bobby knows it's coming up!"

I think back to the cards and the red ribbon. Less than a week until my birthday. A few more days until there's another card, another sentiment for Mama to hide from me.

We walk into school with a minute to spare, and somehow, I don't run into Janet. We'll see each other soon enough. Whatever will be will be, and the good Lord will have my back. I get a drink of water from the fountain outside the principal's office door. Timmy Dugan is also getting a drink, and every time he pushes on his button, the arch of water in my fountain falls lower. The homeroom bell rings, and Timmy finishes drinking, propelling water straight up my nose and all over my face. Janet and Sandra walk by just as I'm wiping it away.

"Just look at her," Janet says. "Clearly, it runs in the family. Making a mess everywhere she goes, just like her mother."

They laugh and walk away with their elbows touching.

"So I got water up my nose. Who cares?" My declaration startles them both and they walk faster.

There's a note on my desk when I get to class. I know instantly it's from Bobby, and I don't try to hide it. I read it right then and there:

Dear Velvet,

I heard about the fight at the pie shop. I don't believe it, but Janet said your mama spit on Mrs. Evans. Did she really do that? If she did, she's got some real courage to take her on. My mom says she's a pain in the keister. Anyway, I just wanted you to know I still like you, and I hope we can go to the movies again soon.

Sincerely,
Bobby

I can't help but giggle. Janet is telling people Mama spit on her mama. Of all the things! I guess that's what you do when you lose—twist the truth around until it looks like your side won.

Dear Bobby,

Yes, there was a bit of an argument. I guess you could say some things needed to be resolved from the past. I know Janet may have said some things, but if she told you my mama spit on her mama, she's telling tales as tall as the flagpole in front of the VFW. If it's OK with you, I'm gonna leave the details of the incident hanging right over the pie counter at Bigsby's. And by the way, I still like you, too.

Sincerely,
Velvet

When class is done, I pass Bobby's desk and hand him the note in front of everyone. Janet lets out a huff, shocked at my sudden boldness. God doesn't like prideful people, but I think he's OK with me standing up to Janet. I smile and walk away. Bobby catches up and joins me on my walk to class. He smells so good, like the park on a spring evening.

"I hear you have a birthday coming up." He smiles like he's got a surprise.

"Yes, I do."

I'm blushing from ear to ear. I just know it.

"How 'bout we go to the movies again this weekend to celebrate? And after, we can go to Bigsby's and get some pie."

My face gets hotter.

"I'm just teasing you, Velvet."

Although I'm relieved, I can't imagine ever going to Bigsby's again, and it makes me sad.

"Excuse me, Bobby," Janet interrupts. "Do you happen to know if our mothers are attending the annual Mother's Day luncheon at church together again this year?"

Bobby looks at me and shrugs his shoulders. "I have no idea, Janet."

I know exactly what Janet is trying to do. She gives him a disappointed look and walks away.

"That was awkward," Bobby says, rolling his eyes.

We say goodbye, and Bobby says he'll write me another note before the day is through. Mercy has to rush home right after school, but I manage to squeeze in a quick report about my day.

"You'll have to let me know what the note says. And if you read more of the journal. And …" she pauses. "If you talk to your mama about the cards."

I touch the note from Bobby in my pocket and decide not to think about the journal, the birthday cards or Mama.

When I get home, the driveway is empty. I could run in and read every single card and the journal if I wanted to. Instead, I walk up to Mary and sit beside her. The sun is shining in patches beneath the willow tree. I pull out the note from Bobby and read it to Mary.

Dear Velvet,
I was wondering if you'd like to be my girl.

Love,
Bobby

Love, Bobby! I close the note tightly, look around to make sure I'm not dreaming, and open it again. Wait until Mercy hears this!

Mama's truck pulls in and stops where the gravel is worn low. She has two bags of groceries.

"What are you doing out here, Velvet?"

"I'm just sitting for a minute."

She has no idea what a day I've had.

"I remember the day Pops brought her home." She smiles and looks at Mary. "He was hell bent on sticking her in the front yard."

"I remember too."

"Any trouble from Janet Evans today?" Mama's eyes peek over the top of the bags.

"Nothing I couldn't handle."

"That's my girl."

I get up, but before I do, I touch Mary's crumbly cement base where her toes should be and think of Pops. Mama hands me a bag to carry in.

The phone rings after dinner, and Mama sounds all business-like.

"That was Mikey Sullivan. He needs me to run over to the shop and grab some papers to bring to Clyde Owen's house for him to sign."

"OK," I say. Yes, Mama. Go ahead and take yourself right over to Clyde Owen's house. The timing couldn't be more perfect.

Once Mama's truck is out of sight, I find the journal under her pillow, right where Mercy and I left it, and the birthday cards.

I hesitate for a second and untie the red ribbon. I open each card like it's made of glass. Inside, every single one is signed, "With all my love, Daddy." And that's it. I study Diamond Jim's cursive—the twists and turns of his handwriting. It's prettier than I'd expect from him. I tie up the cards and push them back under the pillow, out of sight.

I pick up the journal and return to the next entry Mercy and I were reading.

Mama wrote:

Now that I know the heartache of losing a child, I pray there won't be complications this time. I can picture DJ and me swaddling our sweet baby and kissing each other nonstop because we're just so damn happy. He doesn't know I'm pregnant yet. Our relationship is moving at such a fast and glorious pace, but I'd be lying if I said I wasn't concerned about how he'll react to this news. I'm not sure why. He tells me I'm different, special, not like any of the other girls he knows.

I haven't told Ditty and Pops about the baby yet either. I wonder what Pops will think of DJ being the father of his first grandchild. Pops likes DJ enough, but he isn't in love with the idea of him dating his daughter. Pops has been bowling for years, and I'm sure he's heard things about Diamond Jim—stories shared only between men and bowling lanes. I worry about how Pops and Ditty will feel about me being an unwed mother. Truth be told, I don't like it either. I want to marry DJ, and this baby growing inside me is sure to lead to a ring on my finger.

I flip to the next entry:

Tonight, I told DJ about the baby. He said he wanted to take me on a date, and I decided it was finally time. He honked his horn when he arrived, and I looked in the mirror one last time. I had to remind myself to stay calm, to feel him out a little bit, to tell him gently. He greeted me with a kiss and suggested we go to the Hickory for ribs. When the hostess said, "Table for two?" I almost replied, "Table for three." We snuggled into a booth, and the waitress brought DJ a beer and asked what I wanted to drink. DJ said I'd have the same, and when I told her water was fine, he looked confused. As the waitress turned to leave, I couldn't wait a second longer, I told him I had something to tell him. "Have at it, pretty lady," he said as he took a sip of his beer and looked around the restaurant. Before I had a chance, the waitress returned and listed the specials. There were so many, I wanted to scream. I cut her off, told her we'd needed a minute longer. Then I squeezed DJ's hand and said, "Honey, I'm pregnant."

His expression fell. His eyes looked the way they do when he bowls a bad round, only worse. My stomach dropped, and fear quickly replaced joy. I tried to play it cool. "We're having a baby," I told him again, trying to sound enthusiastic, thinking my excitement would rub off on him. After a long pause he finally said, "Pregnant? Are you sure?" I told him yes, 100 percent and reached for his hands, but he kept a tight grip on his beer bottle. I told myself he was just shocked. He asked me what I was going to do about it, and it took all my strength not to start crying. My voice shook as I said, "We're keeping the baby, DJ. I'm keeping the baby." I sat up taller and he gave a small nod, but still, no words came out of his mouth.

When the waitress came back, I said I didn't want anything. I couldn't eat. I felt sick to my stomach. DJ gave her his most charming smile, flirting while he ordered a half rack of ribs. How could he after the news I had just shared? When she left, his smile disappeared again, and he asked when the baby was due. I said the beginning of May and promised it will all work out. "You'll be a wonderful father," I said and touched his leg. I felt him flinch. The word "father" teetered on a thin thread of a tightrope between us. I wondered how God could let this happen. How could he bring a life into the world, knowing full well there was trouble ahead? How could I have been so stupid to ignore the warning signs?

As I sat watching DJ eat, feeling unwanted and unloved, I noticed a tall blonde woman walk into the Hickory like she'd done it a hundred times before. She wore tight black pants and a short-sleeved red shirt with a slit at the neck that showed off her perfect round breasts and the pretty gold chain dangling between them. I know everyone in town, but I didn't recognize her. DJ's eyes locked onto her like he was a hunter, and she was his prey. I watched as he licked barbecue sauce slowly from his fingers and his lips as the booby blonde stared back at him. The betrayal I felt crawled along my skin, burrowed in the darkest part of my heart. Then I watched as DJ, weak in the flesh, winked at her while I sat right there next to him with his baby inside me.

Mikey Sullivan walked into the restaurant just then, and when I saw him, I wanted to run to him. I tried to remember what it felt like to be loved by a good man, a decent man. He caught my gaze, gave me a soft smile and tears bubbled up. Now the handsome man beside me was ugly in my eyes. While others saw a thick head of wavy hair, I saw a matted down mop full of gooey pomade that left my hands sticky. The put-together outfits all the ladies raved about now looked shrunken and silly to me. I felt nothing but disgust. I nearly got sick right on the table.

The headlights from Mama's truck bounce along the wall, and I put the journal back. I run into the bathroom, let the shower run, and cry under the warm water. This is awful. Just awful! My daddy is a terrible man, and I want nothing to do with him … ever! I want to burn those cards. This must be why Mama hid them from me.

I hope she stood up and slapped him across the face. I hope she told him to go to hell. I hope she threw her water on him and the booby blonde watched the whole thing. I cry harder.

After a few minutes, Mama cracks the door open a bit and

says, "I'm home! Velvet, you need to turn on the exhaust fan. It looks like a rain forest in here."

The door closes and I feel even worse. My poor Mama. I stay in the shower until the tears stop flowing, until I can bear the pain enough to put on a brave face for her.

The following day, I tell Mercy about what I read, and I cry all the way to school.

"It's OK, Velvet. She made it through, didn't she?"

I nod my head, but I don't know if that's the correct answer. Mama might be doing better now, but Diamond Jim robbed her of the thing she wanted most—his unconditional love.

CHAPTER 18
FORGIVE

B y the time Mercy and I get to school, I feel a little better. I see Bobby, and he's looking at me like I'm supposed to give him something. The note! He asked me to be his girl, but I didn't respond. I wish I could tell him why I forgot—the journal, the birthday cards, Mama in that booth at the Hickory, the booby blonde, knowing my daddy never really wanted me. But I can't. It's all too much. I find my seat in class and whip out a piece of paper.

Dear Bobby,
Yes! I'd love to be your girl. You're sweet to ask, and I'd love to go to the movies again for my birthday.

Love,
Velvet

I fold the note and put it in my pocket. Do I love Bobby? I think about the way Mama loved Diamond Jim and how she put all her focus on him, and I don't want to be like that. I quickly rewrite the note.

Dear Bobby,

Thank you for asking me to be your girl. The answer is
yes. And I'd love to go to the movies again with you.

Velvet

Not signing the note with anything other than my name
seems rude. I go back and draw a tiny heart next to my name.
Hopefully, it will be good enough for now. Besides, I'm not
ready to make my whole life about anybody.

I give the note to Bobby after class, and he smiles. His
kindness and warmth are so genuine I almost cry right there.
Somehow, I make it through the whole day, forcing back tears
whenever I think about Mama.

After school, I tell Mercy I can't walk home with her.

"Are you OK, Velvet?" she asks.

"Not really," I say. "I just need to do something after school
by myself."

Instead of turning left toward Tender Vine Lane, I go straight.
I see the marquee from two blocks away—it's supposed to say
Strike Zone in red letters, but the Z is burned out, so it says
"Strike one." I walk in the side door, hoping no one will see
me. The place is empty except for the manager, who's arranging
bowling shoes by size, and a young man polishing the lanes.
Mama's favorite, Elvis, plays on the jukebox, and the lights are
low.

I make my way to the hallway by the bathrooms, and I see
Diamond Jim's picture, the third one in the row of champions.
At first, I stand back from it, keeping my distance. But I want

to see up close what Mama saw when she looked into his eyes. I inch forward until I'm eye to eye with Diamond Jim himself. I imagine him winking at the booby blonde. I look closely at his lips and can almost hear him asking Mama, "What are you going to do about it?" when she told him she was pregnant. The question repeats in my mind like a needle skipping on a scratched record.

I stood in this very spot as a little girl, yearning for him. I'd heard his name enough to think he was mine and I was his. But now, all I want is not to be his. I don't want our eyes to be the same shape, our smiles to both tilt to the left. I don't want to be anything like him.

The young man polishing the floors turns the corner and says, "Oh, hi. I didn't know anyone was here. Are you looking to bowl? The lanes won't be ready for another 30 minutes." He has his palm on the door of the men's bathroom and waits for me to respond.

"Um, no," I say. "I was just gonna get something from the vending machine."

He smiles and points to the photos lining the wall. "That there's our wall of winners, the best bowlers the Strike Zone has ever seen."

He doesn't know Strike Zone Champion number three is ugly from the inside out.

"Neat," I say.

He pushes through the bathroom door and disappears behind it.

I move in closer for one last look and whisper, "I'll never

come here again. Do you understand? I used to want to find you, now I pray I never do."

I feel the tears come and I don't know if it's because I'm angry or heartbroken, but my throat burns, and my head throbs. "You didn't deserve Mama. That's probably why she hid the birthday cards from me. She was protecting me from you."

Before I walk away, the words leave my mouth like a stone from a slingshot right between his eyes. "I'll never forgive you. Ever."

I open the ladies' room door, go into the first stall, and dab my eyes with toilet paper. I won't waste these tears on him. I won't! I wash my hands and look in the mirror. "You don't need a daddy, Velvet. You never have."

I take the long way home, clenching my fists and ready to fight. I walk past Our Savior's Bleeding Heart Church, and the message on the marquee from Luke 23:24 makes my feet come to a screeching halt. "Father forgive them, for they know not what they do." Before I know it, I'm walking through the big wooden doors, immersed in all the senses of church, the place I hold most sacred. The stained-glass windows glow from the outside in, the smell of incense lingers in the air, and the Eucharist candle flickers, letting me know I am not alone. I make my way to a pew toward the front, drop to my knees before the altar, and I pray:

Lord, my heart feels heavy. It feels like I've got a rock in my chest. Please tell me how to move on. I've lived my whole life wondering about my daddy and if he loves me, and now I know he didn't even want me.

I unclench my fists and clasp my hands together next to my

heart. Safe within these walls, the tears I've been trying so hard to contain come out. I weep and weep until my chest relaxes and I can hear my breathing again.

Father Matthew slips quietly into the pew in front of me. I shift from kneeling to sitting. He hands me a tissue without looking at me, and we both sit quietly, staring up at the cross.

"He is amazing," Father Matthew says, tilting his head toward Jesus. "He had the heart of a child in all the best ways." Father nods his head, agreeing with himself. "He was slow to anger, quick to forgive, and even as a man, he had childlike faith in the direction his father asked him to go in."

I blow my nose and ask, "How could Jesus forgive the people who hurt him? They were terrible people."

I hear my voice crack and echo through the church when I say the word terrible. I surrender to the hurt. Tears fall and I don't try to stop them.

Father turns and speaks directly to me. "Velvet, he understood that those people didn't know God's love. By forgiving them while they were hurting him, he allowed them to see for themselves how beautiful it is. He gave them a gift—the gift of freedom from their wrongdoings."

"But what if," I choke back more tears, "you can't forgive someone?"

"Pray for peace and clarity. By forgiving someone who has hurt you or others, you give God the space to do his work in you. So pray for the ability to forgive and know it doesn't happen overnight. Give yourself time and watch God work in your heart."

I feel deeply everything Father Matthew is saying. Peace

washes over me and holds me steady. My tears stop, but I continue to pray, I keep asking God for help. Father Matthew walks to the altar and bows in reverence. Then he disappears into the sanctuary, leaving me alone with Jesus.

I notice the light of dusk has changed the way the stained-glass windows glow. I focus on the stations of the cross. The one depicting Jesus' crucifixion shimmers in the setting sun. Unlike how I looked in the eyes of Strike Zone Champion number three, Jesus looks into the eyes of those who sinned against him with compassion and love. I glance at the burning candles and notice the one Mama lit the other day is still burning.

Father Matthew is right, there are no winners in the fight of unforgiveness. I walk out of the church knowing Diamond Jim hurt those around him because he was afraid. I think about how quickly I abandoned him after reading Mama's journal, how I allowed my own fear to exceed his.

I walk back to the trailer park slowly, thinking about what Father said. The town is quiet, and I watch as the men of Sack City come home from work and families sit down for supper. As I make my way to Tender Vine Lane, I see Mama's truck in the driveway.

"Velvet!" I hear someone call my name. "Velvet!"

I realize it's Bobby, across the street at his grandma's house.

"Hi!" he calls out.

"Hi!" I wave back. I compose myself like I haven't been crying my eyes out and on my knees, begging God for help. "What are you doing at your grandma's house on a weeknight?"

I look closer at Mrs. Johnson's house and see her cat, Mr. Jenkins, clawing at the front door.

"It's my grandma's birthday. She wanted us to come over for cake. I was hoping to see you," he says. "I didn't think you were home."

"I am now," I say.

Bobby walks over and stands in front of me. "You OK, Velvet?" The way he tilts his head with concern makes me like him even more. "You didn't seem like yourself today."

"I'm OK, thank you."

It feels weird talking to Bobby with no one else around. My eyes search the grass beneath my feet like I'm looking for something I've lost.

"Good to hear," he says. "So, your birthday ... it's on Saturday, right?"

"Yes." I haven't given it much thought.

"I hope I can still take you to the movies. Mercy and Tommy can come with us again, if you want?"

Bobby looks down at the grass too, like the answer lies somewhere between the blades. Does he want it to be just him and me?

"That sounds nice," I say.

Bobby moves in closer, and my feet feel the way I imagine Mary's do under the willow tree, heavy and stuck in place. This time, he doesn't ask, he leans in and kisses my cheek.

"See you tomorrow, Velvet."

I watch Bobby walk back to his grandma's house, and I turn to the window to see if Mama is watching. Thankfully, she's not. I look up at the sky. The wind is rustling the flags at the entrance to the park. In my mind, I hear Father Matthew's sermon from the other day: "God is in the wind ... You'll feel him when you search for him." I rub the goose bumps on my arms and go inside to find Mama.

CHAPTER 19
SWEET 16

When I went to bed last night, I was 15 years old, and today I woke up a whole year older. Funny thing is, I don't feel much different, but when I stop to think about it, I am. I wonder if Mama looks at me and sees a whole year gone.

I glance out the window and blink as my eyes adjust to the morning light. Hand on my heart, I look outside and start a prayer: *Thank you, Lord, for another birthday* ... But something catches my eye. At first, I think I'm seeing things. There's a green envelope taped to the outside of my bedroom window. I jump out of bed to get a closer look. The word "Velvet" in black ink pulls me closer, like a big flashing neon light.

I squint, trying to make sense of what I'm seeing. Why would Bobby put a note on my bedroom window when he can give it to me at school? I open the window and push against the screen, hoping the envelope falls to the ground. I try to stick my hand under the screen to grab the envelope, but I can't. So I slip into my fuzzy yellow slippers and head outside, wearing my pajama bottoms and an old Hip Joint sweatshirt of Mama's. On my way I pass Ditty, who's whipping up my birthday breakfast in the kitchen.

"Well, look what we have here—our birthday girl! Sixteen years old today!" Ditty comes at me with open arms. I squeeze her quickly and say thank you. "Where on God's green earth are you headed, young lady?"

"I just have to get something outside," I say.

"Don't be too long. Your birthday pancakes will be ready soon."

The grass is cold and dewy, and the moisture seeps through the soles of my slippers. The sun has risen above the trees, and birds of all varieties are singing loudly. Usually, I'd stop and thank God for this, but I'm on a mission to get to that envelope. Once I'm under my window, I realize I won't be able to reach it and look around for something to stand on. There's a milk crate by the front door I can use, and I run back to get it. The smell of Ditty's homemade pancakes wafts out through the front door, and Mama's inside shouting, "Where's the birthday girl?"

I shout back through the screen, "Be right there, Mama."

Ditty answers too. "Velvet is doing something outside, Lynette. Now, come help me with this breakfast."

I wait to see if Mama will respond.

"Something outside?" she asks.

Ditty distracts Mama. I head back to the window, and my heart races as I examine the mysterious green envelope. It's from him. It has to be. Maybe he knows Mama never gave me the birthday cards he picked out for me. I situate the crate under the window and step up on it in my soggy slippers, careful to keep it steady beneath me. It starts to wobble until the weight of my body pushes it deep into the damp earth. I reach up for the envelope, but I can't even snag a corner of it. I stand on my tiptoes, the crate tips forward, and I fall into the side of the mobile home.

I need something taller. I run to the garden shed and find our old blue metal cooler. When I lift it from its surroundings, Pops' shotgun falls from where it's leaning against the wall and startles me. I set it upright and drag the cooler outside to the window. I step up on it. I can finally reach the note, but as I do, my sopping wet slippers slide across the top of the cooler. I right myself and try desperately to reach for the envelope, but I can't, and I don't. Instead, I fall to the ground and land on my arm. Hard.

The shock of hitting the ground takes a few seconds to process. I try to get up, but my arm and wrist hurt something fierce. Tears come as I lie there and yell for Ditty and Mama to come help me. The note dangles by the tiniest piece of tape. I almost had it.

"Mama? Ditty?" I wince.

Ditty comes outside. "Oh, sweet Jesus, what happened?"

I don't apologize to Jesus, 'cause Ditty did call him sweet.

"I fell, and I think I broke my arm."

Ditty rushes over and kneels beside me. Wincing now with every word, I muster, "There's a note on my window." I point up with my good arm. "I was trying to reach it, and I fell." The pain is like a tear generator. "I don't want Mama to see it," I whisper to Ditty.

She grabs hold of my waist and good arm and helps me off the wet ground.

"Ouch, ouch, ouch." I cringe as we make our way to the front door.

Ditty shouts, "Lynette! Lynette!"

The next thing I know, Mama runs outside, freshly showered, wearing her peach robe, her hair in curlers covered with a bright pink shower cap.

"What the hell is going on?" she asks.

"We need to take Velvet to the doctor. I think she broke her arm."

The pain is pulsing from my shoulder to my wrist.

"Sweet Jesus, Velvet! What the hell have you done to yourself?"

Again, with the sweet Jesus.

"I fell."

"I can see that, young lady. It doesn't take a rocket scientist to figure that out! How did you fall?" She doesn't wait for an answer. "Where does it hurt?"

I point to my left wrist, and Mama grimaces like she's the one in pain.

"OK, let me call Marjorie Willows."

Mrs. Willows is a retired nurse who lives a few doors down. Mama fumbles through her directory, her bubblegum pink fingernails making their way down the alphabet. "Here it is!" She pulls the phone and cord away from the wall and with her to the kitchen table.

"Ditty, can you please get me a cup of coffee so I can start making some sense? And get some ice on Velvet's wrist before it swells up."

Ditty grabs a cup and pours coffee for Mama. She cracks ice cubes into a white cotton dish towel, gathers the corners so it's a pouch, and sets it on my wrist. Then she hands me a glass of water and some aspirin, which I gulp down.

"Marjorie? Hi, honey, it's Lynette Underwood. Oh, I've been better. It seems my Velvet has fallen and may have broken her wrist or arm. I know, I know, it's a darn shame. And today is her 16th birthday!"

Mama pauses as she listens to Marjorie while she pulls at her shower cap. "Would you mind coming and taking a quick look at her?" Another pause. "Oh, bless your heart! Thank you, Marjorie."

Mama hangs up the phone and says, "She'll be right over!

"Velvet, would you mind telling me how this happened?" she asks.

I glance at Ditty.

"Our poor birthday girl." Ditty says, rubbing my back.

"There's a note taped to my bedroom window. I was trying to reach for it, and I fell."

The words drop out of my mouth like a roller coaster at the top of a steep hill.

Mama looks at Ditty, who shrugs. Mama tightens her robe and walks outside like a woman on a mission. Ditty follows, and I have no choice but to go, too. We gather by the side of the house, and Mama looks up at the green envelope, her bare feet now covered in wet blades of grass.

Ditty marches to the shed mumbling, "If you wanna get something done, you just gotta take the bull by the horns and do it your damn self."

Sorry for all the cussing, Lord.

Ditty comes back with a broom and swats at the note, and we all watch it fall to the ground in slow motion. Ditty picks it up and shows Mama the handwriting. Mama grabs hold of her heart, her knees buckle, and boom! She hits the ground. Her curlers seem to cushion her landing. I can't lend a hand because the pain in my wrist is intensifying with every passing minute. I look at Ditty, who isn't the slightest bit fazed. She only shakes her head and says, "Aren't we a fine mess this morning," and bends to help Mama. "Lynette, get up. Now."

Mama's eyes are open, but she doesn't move.

Mrs. Willows approaches and sees me and Mama outside in our pajamas. She doesn't ask how I hurt myself or why Mama is lying on the ground, she just gets right to taking care of us while Ditty slides the green envelope into her pocket.

Mrs. Willows says my wrist is broken. Ditty helps Mama to the couch and drives me to the doctor to get a cast. As we sit in the waiting room, I look up and see a picture of an older man on the wall. Beneath the image, it reads "In Loving Memory of Dr. James Dearberg." I wish I could tell Ditty I know him, but I don't. I only feel like I do.

The doctor asks how I hurt myself. When I tell him, he says, "That must have been some important letter." I look at Ditty, who I recall has the envelope in her pocket still. I wait until the doctor steps out of the room.

"Is it from him?" I ask.

I don't want to say his name. Ditty nods her head.

"I know he sends me a birthday card every year, Ditty. I found them in Mama's room."

She rubs my thigh, acknowledging the truth.

"Mrs. Evans must be right. He must be in Sack City. He probably taped it on my window to make sure I got it."

Ditty shifts from side to side in the metal chair beside me, not answering my question.

"Can I see it?"

She looks away for a minute and reluctantly pulls it from her pocket. The envelope is bent and damp but still intact despite all the dramatics. I stare at the front of it like the letters of my name tell a long-lost secret. Ditty scoots closer to me, her chair scraping across the floor. I open the edge of the envelope, careful not to rip what's inside. This time it's not a greeting card, it's a lined index card with black writing on it. *Lord, I don't know what this says and it's making me nervous.* I pull it out and read:

Dear Velvet,
You are 16 today. I hope you have a nice birthday. I think about you often.

With all my love,
Daddy

I read it over and over while Ditty sits patiently beside me. I hand it to her so she can look at the handwriting, but she already knows who wrote it. She reaches out to touch my good arm, and I cringe as if it hurts, too. The nurse comes in, oblivious that my long-lost daddy has contacted me, and sets out the makings of a cast on a tray at the side of my bed. Ditty shoves the card back in the envelope and into her pocket while I sit silently, watching the nurse wrap strips of white mesh coated in white pasty goo around my wrist and arm.

When it's all over, I feel numb. Ditty and I drive home in silence, and every few minutes she reaches over and pats my leg. We pull into the driveway and notice Mama rummaging in the garden shed. When she turns around, we see she is holding Pops' shotgun with a vacant look on her face.

"Stay right here, Velvet," Ditty says firmly.

So I do. I roll down the window and watch from the front seat as Ditty runs to Mama and the two of them engage in a heated conversation. Mama holds the gun like an old pro, just like Pops taught her.

"I'm gonna find that bastard and kill him!" Mama shouts.

Would she really hurt him?

"Not today, Lynette," Ditty says. She plants her feet firmly to the ground and takes hold of the gun.

Mama seems stunned, but not swayed. Ditty walks the shotgun back to the shed and shuts the door. She glances at me before leading Mama into the house. Once they're inside, I slide out of the seat and go sit by Mary. I don't say anything—I don't need to.

CHAPTER 20
DEAR FUTURE HUSBAND

S o much has happened today, and it isn't even over. The phone rings inside, but no one answers it. Ditty is too busy making sure Mama doesn't kill Diamond Jim, and I need a moment with Mary, so I'm still sitting here trying to make sense of it all.

I bet Mercy is trying to call me. The date! She isn't going to believe any of this! Not the letter, my broken wrist, or Mama standing in the yard with a shotgun in her hands. Come to think of it, she may believe that.

Right now, I just want to be right here. I lean my whole body against Mary. My wrist aches and my heart is tired, but I open the green envelope again.

With all my love,
Daddy

I study the letters. I picture him holding the pen. I wonder if his hand hovered above the card as he considered whether it was worth the effort. Or if he quickly pressed ink to paper, without giving it a second thought.

Mama looked like she was ready to kill him. He can't be too

far away. The thought of Diamond Jim being in Sack City makes me shiver. Maybe he stopped and bowled a round at the Strike Zone or popped into Bigsby's for a piece of pie. Mrs. Evans would have loved it if, out of the blue, Diamond Jim sat down at her pie counter. She'd probably be talking about it to everyone in town, "Well, well, well … Guess who came to see me?"

Ditty calls from the kitchen window, interrupting my reenactment of Mrs. Evans bragging to Mary. "Velvet, come on in here, and let's celebrate your birthday the way we're supposed to."

My birthday. I completely forgot. It's late afternoon, and we haven't eaten all day. I put the note back in the envelope and use my good arm and Mary's head for leverage to stand up.

Lord, I'm not sure what to do with all of this. I feel guilty and numb. Please help me, so I know what to do next. And please, please help Mama's heart.

Mama doesn't even notice when I walk in. She looks like she's in a trance, staring straight into the TV as if it holds the answers to all of her problems.

Ditty, forever trying to make everything better, is flipping pancakes on the griddle as bacon sizzles in the skillet.

"Birthday girl, you sit right here." She pulls out a chair and pours me a big glass of orange juice. "We're having breakfast for dinner—I'm calling it brinner—for your birthday. Birthday brinner!"

Ditty makes me smile, and it feels like a hug. Suddenly, I'm starving and devour every morsel she puts in front of me. Mama doesn't come to join us, but Ditty peeks around the corner from time to time to check on her.

"Do you think Mama would hurt him?"

"No, honey. I don't. I think your Mama has a lot of fights in her but not many follow throughs. She's in shock, is all."

"That makes two of us."

Ditty clears my plate and places a chocolate cupcake with a candle on it in front of me. I smile again and thank her.

"Of course, baby girl." She motions for me to move into the living room near Mama and lights the candle. "OK, Lynette, let's sing Happy Birthday to our girl."

We both wait for Mama to respond. When she doesn't, Ditty raises her voice. "Lynette!"

Mama comes to like she's startled awake from a deep sleep.

Ditty starts singing and gives Mama a stern look to get her to sing. Mama chimes in reluctantly. Together they finish it, Ditty stronger than Mama, "Happy birthday, dear Velvet, happy birthday to you!"

Mama watches me intently as I blow out the candle, then asks, "What'd you wish for, Velvet?"

Something about her tone robs me of my moment. I don't want to tell her.

"Nothing," I say.

Ditty hands me my gift from both of them. "Here you go, sugar."

Ditty glares at Mama in a you'd-better-rise-to-the-occasion kind of way, but Mama doesn't flinch.

"A makeup kit with eye shadows, lipsticks, blushes and brushes!" I squeal, "Thank you so much!" I hug Ditty.

"So, what'd ya wish for, Velvet?" Mama asks again, and her pressing the issue sucks the life right out of the room.

I hesitate, holding the makeup kit to my chest.

"I wished I could meet him, you know, if he's still in town."

Mama slams her plate onto the coffee table, sending pieces of pancakes bouncing into the air.

Ditty gasps and shouts, "Lynette Lucille!" like she's scolding a child.

Mama gets up and walks right out the door. Ditty follows to make sure she doesn't go back to the shed, and I turn away, afraid I've betrayed Mama in the worst possible way. Mama hops into the truck and reverses out of the driveway.

"Should we be worried?" I ask.

I can't help it. I feel awful.

"No, sweetheart," Ditty says, picking pancakes up off the floor. "She'll be fine. We've gotta let her fight this one out with herself."

I pull the candle out of my cupcake and unwrap it slowly. Before I take a bite, the phone rings. The date!

"Hello."

"Velvet? I've been trying to reach you all day!"

"I'm sorry, Mercy. You won't believe what happened today." I look down at my cast. "Can you come over?"

"Yes. Is everything OK?"

I pause and look out at the driveway.

"Just come over and I'll tell you everything."

"I'll be right there. Oh, and happy sweet 16!"

Ditty clears our brinner plates. I tell her that Mercy's on her way over and that we were supposed to go on a date.

"Supposed to go on a date? Sweetie, you've got a beat-up wrist, but the rest of you is just fine!" Ditty holds my cheek in her palm and then lifts my chin. "You girls go and have a nice time tonight. It's your birthday!"

"I'm worried about Mama."

"Don't be, honey. I'll be here when your Mama gets back. She can't get into too much trouble with me around."

Mercy walks through the front door less than three minutes after we hung up the phone. I clear my throat and she notices my cast.

"Sweet Lord ... What happened, Velvet?"

I tell her everything and hand her the green envelope to read for herself.

She shakes her head, unable to speak, and gives me a big hug. "That is quite a birthday."

Ditty chimes in, "She'll be in the cast for a few weeks."

"I want to be the first one to sign it!" Mercy says, and whispers, "Are we still going on a date?"

She rummages through the junk drawer in the kitchen for a pen.

"I know all about the date," Ditty says. "And I think you two should go and have some fun." She sets out some aspirin. "Take these before you go, sweetie."

I smile at Mercy and pick up the aspirin. "Looks like we're going on a real date!"

Mercy and I run to my room to get ready. I pull out my new makeup kit and show Mercy all the colors.

"It's so pretty," she says.

"Isn't it? I don't even want to use it." But we do.

Next I look for something to wear that says, "it's my birthday!" But it's hard. My new cast makes everything look weird. Every once in a while, I glance at the green envelope to make sure it's still there. *Lord, no more running from the past. No more hiding.*

I hear Mama pull back onto the gravel, come inside, make her way into the kitchen and pour herself a glass of wine. Of course, she went to the liquor store. Why can't it be about me right now? Shouldn't she be happy Diamond Jim wants me to know about him? Why does it always end up being all about her?

I put on my cream-colored sundress and drape a sweater over my shoulders 'cause it won't fit over my cast. Mercy says I look pretty, and I trust her. I'm ready to get out of here, away from Mama. I think about seeing Diamond Jim in town. What would I even do?

"Where do you think he is?" Mercy asks, as if reading my thoughts.

"I don't think he could be too far." I look out my window, like he's hiding in a bush.

"Maybe, instead of seeing a movie, we could go bowling instead?" I say, surprising myself.

Mercy nods her head vigorously, and I feel like Nancy Drew about to solve a mystery.

"We're supposed to meet the boys at the theater at 6:30. Before they buy the tickets, let's tell them the new plan. Your daddy might be at the bowling alley, Velvet!"

I picture the Strike Zone Champ standing in the hallway by the bathrooms, admiring his picture.

As we leave, I don't engage with Mama. I shout at the house instead of her, "We're leaving now!"

Ditty is washing dishes. "OK, girls," she calls out. "Have a nice time, and be gentle with your wrist, Velvet."

We make it to the theater before the boys do, and I search the streets for Diamond Jim. I've studied his picture enough to know what his face looks like, and Mama has described his body plenty of times. I bet I could pick him out in a crowd. He must have driven down Main Street many times. I picture him cruising in his shiny black Cadillac. He feels close and far away at the same time, and I have trouble focusing on what Mercy is saying.

Bobby and Tommy arrive and look surprised to see us there so early. Bobby notices my cast right away.

"What happened, Velvet?" He's so shocked he forgets to wish me a happy birthday.

"I fell and broke my wrist, and it was really stupid." I'm not ready to tell him the whole story.

"I'm sorry," he says. "Happy birthday!"

He smiles and hands me a white flower.

"Thank you!" I pluck the end of the stem off and stick it behind my ear. Like magic I forget about the ache in my wrist and remember I'm officially 16.

The boys walk toward the ticket counter, and Mercy stops them. "We were thinking about going bowling instead of seeing a movie. Would that be OK?"

They look at each other. "Sure," they say in unison.

"What about your wrist, Velvet?" Bobby asks.

"It'll be OK."

The four of us walk to the Strike Zone, and every few minutes I look behind me, around corners, and in between buildings. I pause when I see a tall man with dark hair, but it's only Sam, the owner of the hardware store, locking up.

It's Saturday night and it seems like the whole town decided to go bowling. I look anxiously around the room, but I don't see him. Bobby and Tommy head to the counter to put our name on the list for a lane, and Mercy goes to get our shoes.

"I'll be right back," I whisper to her. I head to the ladies' room, down the hallway of champs. This time, I don't bother pretending I have other business there. I stop and look right at him. He was here today. I know he was. I walk to the counter where the boys stood minutes earlier.

"Can I help you?" the manager asks.

He talked to Diamond Jim today, I know it. Diamond Jim stood right where I'm standing now.

"Do you need a lane?" The manager raises one eyebrow.

"No, thank you." I leave the counter and find Mercy. "He was here. I know it. Something in my body is telling me."

Mercy nods. "That's called intuition. It's your inner wisdom. Yours must be strong."

I walk back to the hallway and look straight ahead at the men's bathroom door like I bet Diamond Jim did earlier. I press my hand on the door until a man approaches from behind me.

"Excuse me, young lady, you've got the wrong room."

What are you doing, Velvet? Who cares if he used this restroom today or any day? I step aside and let him enter. I return to my friends. Bobby is fussing with the bowling balls, Tommy is setting up the scorecard, and Mercy has my shoes laid out on a bench.

"You OK, Velvet?" Bobby asks.

"Yes, thanks. I guess I'm still a little shaken up from falling."

This isn't a lie. My wrist aches and my head throbs. We bowl a few rounds, but my balance is off with the cast and all, and I can't stop looking around to see if Diamond Jim is here.

Bobby whispers, "We don't have to bowl if you don't want to. I mean, you are kinda beat up." He looks at my cast sweetly.

I agree and we all decide to leave. When we get to the door, I look back at Mercy and she smiles at me. I scan the bowling alley one last time. Bobby holds the door open for me, and when the fresh air hits my skin, my shoulders relax. We sit on the curb, and he asks, "Are you sure you're OK, Velvet?"

I look into his eyes and say, "No, I'm not." I choke up, and he scoots closer to me. How does he know what to do? "My daddy ... He left a note for me this morning for my birthday and ... well ... I've never met or spoken to him." The words out loud sound so sad. "He left when I was a baby."

Bobby reaches for my hand. "I kinda knew your story. You know, small town talk."

I nod. I get it. Everyone knows.

"It's nice he wrote you, though, right?" Bobby searches my face for a reaction.

Nice? I honestly don't know. It feels more like an unwanted interruption, like when you're watching a TV show and there's an emergency drill, the picture goes fuzzy, and it makes a horrible buzzing alarm sound.

"It's nice, I guess, but I'm really confused. My mama got real upset about it and now I'm worried about her, too."

Bobby and I walk toward the empty swings at the park across the street like they're calling our names. I hold on to one chain with my good hand, wrap my elbow around the other chain, and use my feet to start moving. Dirt gathers in my sandals as I push into the freedom of the breeze. My sweater lifts and lowers against my back. Despite my worries, my stomach bounces with joy. I turn to Bobby and smile. He asks if I want to sit on the hill. He wants to kiss me again, I can tell, but I'm not sure how I feel about it. Is this what 16-year-olds do?

"Sure," I say, with all the "I'm a year older" confidence I can muster.

Bobby takes my hand as we walk. The hill overlooks Main Street, and the spring air is warm but crisp. As I straighten my sweater, Bobby helps place it evenly on my shoulders, and then he kisses me. At first, it's like it was when we were at the movies, a small peck. A "hey, hi, I'm right here and I like you" kind of kiss. But then he scoots closer, and his lips linger longer. I let go, let myself enjoy the moment like I did when I was on the swing, and snuggle in by his side. I close my eyes, and our lips find each other. It's easy to kiss him. Every touch of his lips dulls the pain in my wrist and lessens my worries.

I don't know what do with my arms, one of them wrapped in plaster and all, so I keep my hands in my lap. Bobby wraps his around my waist. It feels good, and I slide in closer. I'm waiting for him to put his tongue in my mouth. I've heard that's what happens next, and I know it's coming. *Lord, please help me do this right.* I don't know if God answers my prayer, but it happens, and I know exactly how to do it. It's not as gross as I thought it'd be. Bobby is gentle and goes slow, making me want to kiss him even more.

Mercy and Tommy walk up the hill. I don't want the night

to end. Time has a funny way of moving quickly when you're having the best time, when you're experiencing the most momentous night of your life.

"Velvet, we better be going," Mercy says.

Bobby squeezes my good hand and helps me up off the ground.

"Coming!" I say.

My lips feel chapped and warm. Mercy looks at me—her eyes smiling and her lips smirking. She knows something big happened. After we say goodbye to the boys and make our way home, I tell Mercy everything. Tommy didn't French kiss her, but he was close.

"Maybe next time," I say like I'm now the expert.

Before I go inside the house, I spend time outside with Mary. "Is it wrong to feel like this?" I ask her.

Mama is asleep on the couch, and I enter the house quietly. I turn off the TV and the lights but leave Mama and her empty glass in the living room. Ditty left two aspirins and a note on the table for me, saying she hoped I had a good time.

Before I go into my room, I glance toward Mama's room. It's been one heck of a day and I'm so tired. But even as I tell myself to go to bed, my legs lead me to the journal.

It's been weeks since I last wrote in here. Maybe that's because when you put something in writing that makes it true.

DJ made it very clear he didn't want anything to do with the baby. He said he didn't sign up for it and dropped me off at home alone. The car ride from the Hickory felt like an eternity, the Cadillac felt like a hearse carrying a dead heart. I wasn't sure if it was mine or his. There was no big goodbye. There was nothing else to say. I certainly wasn't about to break down and cry in front of him or beg for him to come to his senses like other women would. I'm not other women. He's a rat. And I should have smelled it long before I let him get inside me.

Then just like that, Diamond Jim, with his swagger and finesse, was gone. My body buckled to the floor once I got inside the front door and tears flowed, burning trails against my skin. I pounded the floor so hard with my fists that the critters living beneath the house surely scattered and ran for safety.

My daddy didn't want me. I think about what Father Matthew said about forgiveness, and I reach up to wipe my eye. I forget about my wrist and bump my cast against my face. I flip the page to the next journal entry:

My belly is getting bigger and so is my heart. God put something more beautiful in my life than a man to love. Now all my love is directed at the sweet babe growing like a wildflower inside me. I'm as big as a house now! Sometimes when I'm out walking, I'll feel the baby move inside me, and it stops me in my tracks. I don't want to miss a single moment. I'll find a spot to sit, put my hands on my belly and feel it doing somersaults. It puts a big smile on my face. I'm thankful this baby is staying put, unlike its daddy, who never returned. But it doesn't matter now, I've got a new love.

Pops and Ditty have been by my side the whole time. Pops tells me regularly he wants to kill Diamond Jim, and I just keep saying, "He ain't worth it, Pops." And it's true. I've been staying home more than I used to 'cause the people of Sack City give me funny looks. Being pregnant and unwed in a small town is hard, but it really only bothers me when I see Mikey Sullivan and the disappointed look on his face. He always stares at the ground like he did something wrong instead of looking me in the eyes. I'm not sure why, he couldn't have saved me from Diamond Jim. No one could have. I pushed God aside and was steering my own life, trusting only myself. Now I thank God for the one good thing that came from it, the one blessing that makes my heart still beat.

My daddy may not have wanted me, but Mama did. She loved me from the very start. I think about doing gymnastics in her belly, and it makes me smile. I turn to the next entry:

I hate him. I hate him. And I'm not sorry. Do you hear what I'm saying, God? I'M NOT SORRY! How could he leave us? The baby is coming any day and where is he? Nowhere to be found. No one has seen him. It's like he disappeared, never existed. I feel like such a fool for thinking he'd come to his senses. I need him, but I don't want him. I miss him, but I don't want to see him. I love him.

I close the journal. Mama has taken me on a roller coaster of emotions. I'm tired of it. And just plain tired. It's time for me to finally go to bed. And then a folded piece of paper falls from between the pages of the journal. I unfold it carefully and read:

Dear Future Husband,

I pray you show up in a car that's not flashy. I pray it's not big and shiny and my eyes aren't drawn to the way it sparkles when the sun hits it just right. I pray the interior is cold and stiff, nothing any woman would want to lay her naked body against. I pray it's an average car, one you'd take to the store to fill the trunk with groceries.

I pray your name is Bob or Carl or Dan, something honest and straightforward. For the love of God, please don't use Brave Bob or Crazy Carl or Dazzling Dan. A name shouldn't make someone think twice or wince or smirk when they say it out loud.

I pray your hair isn't stuck in one place like a helmet on your head. I pray it's naturally soft and smooth, and there are no bottles of hair tonics cluttering the bathroom counter. I pray your scent is fresh like a shower and soap, rather than dime store cologne. And rather than slick outfits and gaudy jewelry, I pray you dress comfortably and casually, and the only jewelry you wear is a wedding ring quietly proclaiming your heart is mine.

I pray you aren't afraid to work hard and feel proud of the money you earn. I pray you think of me, miss me, and want to get home to me while you work. I pray the women of Sack City notice you but don't chase after you because they know, without a doubt, they don't stand a chance of winning your affection because you love me with your whole heart.

I pray you love my family. And I pray when it comes to loving my daughter, who was conceived in the back of a show-off car with a show-off man who had a show-off name, you will make her yours, despite who and where she came from. I pray when she's older, you'll make time for her, you'll help her with homework, you'll talk to her about boys, and teach her what to look for in a good one. I pray you'll cherish her so much you'll tell her the moon and the stars were made just for her.

I pray you never forget what I told you about all the nights I spent alone, looking at the empty side of my bed, waiting for someone like you to come along. I pray when you think about me raising my girl without a daddy, you will squeeze me a little tighter, kiss me a little longer, and assure me with your calming presence that you will always stay.

Hoping you get here soon,
Lynette

I turn the letter over and see inky scribbles on the back. When I squint, I can see what Mama scribbled over. It says, "Dear Mikey." Mikey Sullivan? Maybe it's not too late for Mama to find love. *Lord, could Mr. Sullivan be Mama's future husband?* I fold the letter and tuck it back between the pages.

I crawl into bed, fluff my pillow, and look out the window. I pray: *Lord, I'm 16, and this has been a day. Don't get me wrong, I'm thankful for it—for the note, for Mama, for Ditty, for Mercy. And Bobby, Lord, I liked kissing him. He's kind and sweet.* I press my fingers to my lips and smile at the thought of Bobby. *Sorry, Lord. I pray Mama finds a new kind of love, the kind she wrote about in her letter, the kind she deserves. I love you and I trust you completely. Amen.*

CHAPTER 21
RED HIGH HEELS

On Monday, everyone at school asks what happened to my wrist, and I don't have a good excuse. I don't want to tell them about the note from my daddy. But why am I protecting him? Maybe he knows Mama has been hiding the cards all these years. Maybe he's trying to make things right. Maybe he wants to get to know his daughter. Maybe he wants me to know he's near. So I tell everyone I tripped on my front steps and landed on my wrist. *Sorry for lying, Lord. Deep down, I know you understand.*

I try to distract myself from all the talk about my cast by paying extra attention in my classes. In English, Mrs. Holden has a special announcement. She's wearing a black skirt, and as Mama would say, "sensible shoes that don't make any sense 'cause they're uglier than sin."

"Mother's Day is next Sunday," Mrs. Holden addresses the class. "With such a special day just around the corner, we're going to try our hand at a short story or a poem about our mothers. The subject of our writing today is: What makes your mother beautiful?"

Everyone in class pulls out pencils and paper, eager to write down all the lovely things they see in their moms. I look over at Janet, and she's already writing in cursive, her hand flowing up and down in a pretty little rhythm on the page, probably saying how wonderful and kind and honest her mother is. Blah, blah, blah! The kid next to me seems to be writing a poem 'cause the lines of words on his paper are taking the shape of a sonnet.

I start with one word: "Mama." I can't think of anything to write. I think about the way she walked into the kitchen just this morning. Even though she spent another night of drinking on the couch, even though my daddy's resurfacing after all this time sent her into a tailspin, something about seeing Mama in the kitchen every morning brings a glimmer of hope. She approaches her daily routine as if the night before, and the night before that, never even happened. There's something about the way she pours water into the coffeepot, fiddles with the coffee can, stands on her tiptoes to reach for a cup, and sits at the kitchen table sipping her coffee that brings me comfort.

Still, I don't know what to write. I twirl my pen and think back further than this morning. I relive moments of Mama's life in my mind: the time she buried her first child in the garden; the time she told Diamond Jim she was pregnant with me; the time she wrote a letter to her future husband; every time she lights a single candle during Sunday Mass; the time she confronted Mrs. Evans at the pie shop; the time she stood in the driveway with Pops' shotgun.

Then it comes to me, and I write:

Red High Heels

She doesn't care about the weather
She'll wear high heels in the rain, the sleet and the snow
Red, 'cause it's her favorite color
"Shoes make a woman, Velvet—remember that"
I will
She danced in those shoes
A million times
Swirling, bending, tapping the stage
Holding her in a memory from long ago
Now when her makeup is done
She reaches for them
The finishing touch
The grand finale
The big show
I watch her buckle one and then the other
Tightening the straps around her ankles
Holding her in the present
She stands up tall
Puts one foot in front of the other
Pauses, stands still, like there's glue keeping her stuck
Another try
She lifts one foot and then the other
Click, click, her heels click against the floor
She's moving forward, forward, forward
Her final click, right out the door
Alone but alive

Down but not beaten
Bruised but not broken
Mama in her pretty high heels

When everyone has finished writing, Mrs. Holden asks if anyone would like to read and scans the room. Janet raises her hand like she's just won bingo for the first time. "Janet, why don't you start, dear?"

Janet stands at the front of the class and clears her throat. "Mother, you are like a beautiful rainbow, filled with the colors of the world. A world you create every day for me. A perfect, sunshiny place for me to grow and explore the goodness of this life."

Janet looks so smug standing up there. If Mama heard this, she would mutter what a crock of sunshiny you-know-what it is. *Lord, I know, I know. I'm being spiteful. Help me to be kinder. And quickly, if you can.*

Janet continues, "Mother, you know how to behave like a woman. Perfect in your posture, dress and tone. You'd never start a fight, you have too much class. Thank you for teaching me how to be a proper lady."

Janet looks at me and I glare right back. I hold my ground. Mama once said, "Velvet, if you're ever alone and staring down an animal, wait for it to look away first. Show it who's in charge." Even though Janet's not an animal, it seems worthwhile to try on her.

Thankfully, Mrs. Holden interrupts. "Thank you, Janet. That was lovely. I'm certain your mother will adore it. Anyone else?"

A few other people get up to read, and I consider it, but I decide to save mine for Mama.

Bobby waits for me after school like the older kids who are going steady do.

"Hi," he says. "How was your first day at school with a cast on?"

I lift my arm to show him the signatures covering it from top to bottom. I'm still nervous around him, which is weird. You'd think after you've touched tongues with someone, all the awkward small talk would be easier, but it isn't. I still never know if I'm doing any of it right.

Mercy is waiting for me, so I tell Bobby I better get going. He turns and waves in her direction. "See ya later, Velvet."

He touches my shoulder, and my stomach tingles.

"See ya later," I say back and try not to smile so big.

Mercy wants to take a long way home today, so we can linger on the corner and talk about nonsense while we wait for her new crush, Jeremy, to appear. Mercy decided Tommy is just a good friend instead of a boyfriend. I think it's 'cause he didn't try to French kiss her at the park, but she says, "There's just no chemistry." She met Jeremy when her daddy was getting his oil changed at Sullivan's Auto Body a few weeks ago. Jeremy lives 25 minutes away and takes the bus every day to work at the auto body shop with Mr. Sullivan and Mama. Mama says, "He's 17 and real nice."

As we approach the shop, I see Mr. Sullivan walk out of the office to talk to a customer and Mama behind him in her high heels, holding paperwork. They look like they could be a married couple running a small business.

"Let's go say hi, Mercy."

I drag her across the street before she has time to primp for Jeremy.

"Oh, OK." Mercy hurries to keep up with me.

"Hello, Mr. Sullivan," I say.

"Hi there," Mercy says awkwardly, looking past Mr. Sullivan toward the garage.

"Well, hello to you both." Mr. Sullivan wipes the oil off his hands onto his denim jumpsuit and adds, "Sorry to hear about your wrist, Velvet. Your Mama said you took quite a tumble."

"Thank you. Yes. I thought I saw my pretty Mama run out here, so I came over to say hi."

I think the reference to my "pretty mama" was a nice touch.

"She's around here somewhere. She's probably inside packing up for the day." He motions to the office.

"OK, I'll see her at home. Mercy needs to get going."

Mercy gives me a confused look. I grab her arm and start walking and then turn and shout, "Mr. Sullivan, you should ask my mama to make you her famous pot roast for dinner some time! I know she'd love to cook for you! Maybe this weekend!"

The words spill out of my mouth the way rubbish overflows from the trash cans at the state fair. I pull Mercy along.

"OK then," Mr. Sullivan says with a nervous laugh. "See you later, girls."

"Nice seeing you, Mr. Sullivan," Mercy says before we cross the street and leave him in the wake of my invite.

"What in the heck just happened, Velvet?"

"Just keep walking."

"I didn't even get to see Jeremy," Mercy pouts.

"You'll see him next time."

"Next time? What do you have brewing?"

I tell Mercy about Mama's letter to her future husband, and that I believe Mr. Sullivan is her one true love. Mercy loves Mama, a good love story, and a mission, which helps her quickly get over not seeing Jeremy.

When Mama gets home from work, she finds me in my room. It's the first time she's spoken to me directly since Diamond Jim left the note, which is now sitting on my dresser. I hope she doesn't notice it.

"Young lady, did you tell Mikey Sullivan today that I would love to make him pot roast?" She's grinning oddly.

"Maybe," I say, trying not to smile. Then, in a rush, I add, "Mama, I think he likes you. I mean, really likes you!"

Mama looks at me like I've gone mad. "Child, I think you may have broken your head, along with your wrist."

"Mama, I see the way he looks at you. You just need to see it for yourself."

"Mikey and I dated when we were just kids. He's moved on now." Mama pulls her hair back like she's about to put it in a ponytail, but she doesn't have anything to tie it with. "Besides, I think he's sweet on my old friend Jenny from the Hip Joint now."

"Did you ever really love him?" I blurt.

Mama lets her hair down. "I did, sure. It was a schoolgirl kind of love. Mikey is a nice man, a good man."

I think about the letter she wrote to her future husband. In it, all she wanted was a good man.

"So?" I say.

"So what, Velvet? That was a long time ago. That ship has sailed."

"Remember when you used to say, 'Velvet, we can buy that when my ship comes in?'"

"Uh-huh." Mama sighs.

"Well, guess what?"

Mama's eyes widen, and she tries to hide another sly grin. I can tell she likes my eagerness 'cause she's still here listening to me, and she's standing a little taller than she was before. I'm so confident in my statement I stand up on my bed like the Holy Spirit has just revived me. I lift my broken wrist and wave my clunky cast in the air. "Your ship came in a long time ago, and it was him! It was Mr. Sullivan!"

Father Matthew says God uses people to get his work done, and by the grace of God almighty, I am doing his work right now.

Mama turns to leave, and without thinking, I shout, "He's your future husband, Mama!"

Mama stops and holds onto the door frame like the whole house will fall if she doesn't. But instead of turning back to see the panicked look on my face, she walks off mumbling that I've lost my mind. I let out a sigh of relief and flop onto my bed. *Lord, I pray I didn't ruin it all.*

CHAPTER 22
BETTY BINGO

M other's Day usually consists of Ditty coming over and making a savory chicken or some other kind of meat that cooks for hours and smells so good my taste buds get cranky waiting for it to come out of the oven. This Mother's Day is different because Ditty is keeping a closer eye on Mama. Today, she's invited Mama and me to play afternoon bingo at the VFW.

"Ladies, the hall is putting on a special bingo just for Mother's Day, and I want us all to go." Ditty holds up her lucky bingo bag and waits for a response.

I turn to Mama, who taps her fingernail against the side of her cup, as if it may disrupt her own plans today to find Diamond Jim and kill him. But she surprises us both by throwing her arms in the air. "Oh, what the hell."

"That's the spirit, Lynette!" Ditty says. "And, Velvet, now that you're of age, you can play your own cards! I'm so happy to have my lucky charm back, even if you are a little broken."

Ditty rubs my cast, and we begin to strategize.

"We can use matching blotters!" I squeal.

Mama gets up and hugs Ditty. "Happy Mother's Day, Mama."

This seems like the perfect moment for me to share my poem with Mama. I run and grab it from my book bag in my room and catch a glimpse of something on my unmade bed. I look closer and see it's the stack of birthday cards from my daddy tied with red ribbon. There's a note with Mama's handwriting:

Velvet,
I'm sorry it took me so long to give these to you. It was wrong of me to keep them from you.

Mama

I pick up the bundle of Hallmark greetings, and my instinct is to hide them. Then I remember that Mama doesn't know I already found them. I reread her note. Why does she think it's time to come clean all of a sudden? I walk back to the living room with the cards. Ditty sees me before Mama does and clears her throat.

Mama looks up with a sheepish look of deep regret.

"Why didn't you ever show me these? I've wondered if he ever asked about me, but I was too afraid to ask, too afraid I'd hurt you."

Mama looks at Ditty for support, and I wonder if Ditty knew about the cards too.

"Sweetie, I guess …" Mama pauses and looks down at her pink toes, "I wanted to hurt him by not giving him the chance to know you."

Regret wells heavy, and Mama lets tears fall over her unwashed "Perfectly Peach" blush from the day before. Ditty comes to the rescue and rubs Mama's shoulders. I sit down and place the cards in the middle of the table. Now I get the saying, "the elephant in the room," but in our case it's bigger and more like the elephant in the mobile home.

I feel bad for not wanting to fix the situation. I could say, "It's OK, don't worry, Mama." I could take the opportunity to tell her about the journal, to come clean. I could confess what I know, but I don't. Instead, I sit at the table holding secrets while Mama cries tears of remorse, and my daddy's sentiments sit like a boulder on our little wooden table, heavy enough to crush it and send splinters flying everywhere.

"Now, let's put the past where it belongs, shall we?" Ditty scoops up the cards and sets them on the kitchen counter, away from Mama and me. "There's been a lot of pain and a lot of hurt these past two days, and one cure I know for sadness is a good ol' fashion game of bingo."

My belly erupts in laughter like if it didn't, I'd die of heartbreak. I laugh so hard my insides ache. Mama giggles nervously, wiping her tears with the edge of her robe, and Ditty, who thinks it's because of what she had said, laughs too. The elephant in the mobile home is replaced by three cackling hyenas trying not to pee our pants in the middle of the kitchen. The laughter breaks through the sad spots and makes room for more.

"I wrote this for you at school, Mama." I hand her the poem.

"You wrote this? For me?" Mama opens it as if something might jump out and scare her.

"Read it, Lynette." Ditty says.

Mama straightens her back and clears her throat. "'Red

High Heels,' by Velvet Underwood," she says smiling. "Well, I certainly love the title." She continues reading. When she gets to the part that says red is her favorite color, she says, "This is true." At the part about her dancing shoes, she pauses for a minute, like she's thinking back to being on stage. She gets to the end, "Alone but alive … Down but not beaten … Bruised but not broken … Mama in her pretty high heels." Her heavy tears from moments earlier are lighter now, dropping from her eyes the way apple blossom petals fall from the trees in the spring. Mama folds the poem with care. "I love it. It's perfect. Thank you, sweetheart."

I stand to hug her, and she wraps me in the silkiness of her robe.

Ditty interrupts our embrace. "Well, wasn't that lovely? Now, let's go play some bingo!"

We arrive at the bingo hall just before the game begins. "Happy Mother's Day" wishes echo through the smoky room. It's set up like a school cafeteria, with 20 to 30 long tables—the kind with attached benches—arranged in horizontal rows.

"There's Betty Bingo," Ditty says.

Betty Williams controls the bingo basket, and Ditty calls her Betty Bingo—but not to her face. Betty is frumpy with a bad perm and reminds me of a grumpy cat. Ditty says she is kind of a dud. "You know, someone who doesn't have a lot of excitement in her life." Poor Betty Bingo.

Ditty buys me my very first bingo cards and informs Betty, "Velvet is officially old enough to play now."

Not interested, Betty nods her head while counting out our cards.

"I feel lucky," Ditty whispers into my ear as we sit down to play.

Mama is already at the table with a distant look in her eyes.

"What is it, Mama?" I ask.

She squirms in her seat, "Oh, nothing." She rearranges the cards that Ditty sets in front of her.

Ditty walks over to the table where the coffee is set up, and I follow her. "Did my daddy used to play bingo here with Mama?"

"He did a few times," she says. "The bingo ladies all loved him. He'd flirt and tell them how lucky they were going to be because he was there. He was a real charmer."

Ditty's friends come over to the coffee table to greet me and ask about my cast. Ditty assures them all that I'm just fine. Louise says, "Oh, sweet Jesus! Thank goodness Velvet is back! Now, come sit by your Aunt Louise."

Lord, I could apologize for the rest of my life and still not keep up with all the times somebody says "sweet Jesus."

Ditty nods like it's OK for me to sit by Louise but whispers in my ear, "Now don't you go rubbing any luck on anybody else, especially Louise."

"I'll save all my special luck just for you," I whisper and find my way back to Mama, who's focused on her cards.

Mama lights a cigarette, and I watch the smoke join the thick cloud that hovers over the rest of the tables. Betty Bingo takes her stand behind the bingo machine. I love the anticipation right after Betty rolls the basket and hands the lucky ball to the announcer. The announcer is usually Sam from the hardware store, but today it's his younger brother, Jerry, who's wearing a bright floral Hawaiian shirt. Jerry asks a last-minute question to the lady in charge of setting up the room. He pulls the microphone closer to him, and the speakers crackle with a high pitch warble, causing everyone to mumble in discomfort. It throws Ditty into a panic.

"Check one-two. Check one-two." The warble fades, and Jerry nods to Betty indicating everything seems to be in working order.

"Where in the hell is Sam?" I hear Ditty stirring the pot with the other ladies around her.

"He must be sick today," one says.

"I heard he sprained his foot, tripped on a watering can that fell off a shelf at the store," another shouts.

"No, no, he's at the retirement home, visiting his mother," another says.

Ditty spreads her cards out in an unsettling way. She'd prefer if everything was the same as it was the last time she played. Now that Sam is gone and Jerry is in his place, she is working herself into a full-blown tizzy. She closes her eyes, and by golly, I think she's saying a prayer.

It's not uncommon to see people praying at bingo. I guess when you want something bad enough, prayer seems to be the logical choice. But I think it's silly to pray to God to win something. I mean, isn't he too busy saving souls and healing people's broken hearts to worry about whether Betty Bingo rolls your winning number? I wonder if he hears these prayers coming from the VFW in the middle of Sack City and just giggles. Or maybe it makes him hoppin' mad. I don't know if God gets angry like that, but I assume sometimes he gets frustrated that people don't see the big picture.

Most players bring good luck charms that they set up in front of their cards. I've seen pocket watches, jewelry, pictures of grandkids, stuffed animals, ashtrays, Jesus figurines and crosses. Ditty always plays with a mini statue of the Virgin Mary that Pops gave her and a lucky handkerchief. And me, of course.

Betty rolls the metal basket of letters and numbers, and everyone looks intently at their cards. Before every ball is rolled, Ditty mutters, "Come on now, Betty Bingo, let's get us a good one." She turns to me and says, "Pay attention, Velvet."

"G48 ..." Jerry calls out and pauses. "N31 ..." Pause. "O64 ..." Pause. Jerry announces them as fast as Betty can produce them, and Ditty frantically searches her 15 bingo cards while my eyes work overtime, trying to keep up with my measly four cards. I see Ditty missed a B2 on card five, and I point to it between calls.

"Good eye, honey," she says.

Then, without any warning, Louise lifts her butt off the bench and shouts bingo, which rattles us all. In her excitement, she accidentally knocks down Ditty's mini statue of Mary. Ditty lets out a small gasp, and I quickly stand Mary upright, which makes Mama chuckle.

Bingo Betty hears the call, and everything stops. Betty checks the winning card, and sure enough, Louise has won $55! Ditty rolls her eyes but then composes herself in time to offer the fakest of congratulations.

"Must be the purple blotters you're using," Ditty says to Louise, who adjusts her light pink shirt and settles back in her seat.

Used cards are discarded, and players get new cards. This

continues for a few more rounds. None of the Underwoods are having much luck today.

"Last game will be a blackout," Jerry announces.

I look at Ditty, confused. She leans in to tell me, "That means you need to fill the whole card!"

Jerry adds, "And, to make it even more interesting, let's make this one a quickie."

"What's a quickie?" I ask Ditty.

"It's speed bingo. Get ready."

And, just like that, we're off and running. Betty Bingo looks like she's working up a sweat rolling the balls and reaching for them as quickly as she can. Jerry talks like he's an auctioneer, fast and loud, "O75, N36, G51, B13, N42, I16." Everyone's eyes move at a furious pace. When Jerry calls out B11, Ditty yells, "Sweet Jesus! Bingo!"

Everyone gasps, and Mama and I laugh. Ditty beams, grabs hold of her statue and kisses the top of Mary's head. I jump to hug Ditty, and then Mama. It's nice to be together on Mother's Day, even in a smoked filled, poorly lit room.

CHAPTER 23
DEAR DIAMOND JIM

I have a funny feeling my poem and my pep talk about Mr. Sullivan are helping Mama feel better. It's not as dramatic as doctors on TV when they use those big metal shockers on a person's chest and jolt them back to life. It's more like my words were an oxygen mask making it easier for her to breathe. If she sees Mr. Sullivan as a possibility, maybe she'll see a future outside her heartache. I know I have a lot more work to do, but I believe the oxygen worked a little.

Whenever I'm alone with her, I want to ask a million questions. Why would Diamond Jim send me all those cards but never come to the front door to see me? Do you think he's still in town? Couldn't we go and find him? But I'm afraid to ask, so I sit beside her as I've always done, rooting for her.

Still, I can't stop thinking about Diamond Jim and wondering if he's in Sack City. The green envelope on my birthday and stack of old birthday cards are a reminder he's close. Without overthinking, I pull out my journal and write:

Dear Daddy ...

It sounds weird, so I start on a new page. I tap my pen against my lip. There's so much I want to say, but I can't seem to get it out.

Dear Diamond Jim,
Thank you for the birthday note, and all the other cards
too. I'd like to meet you.

Sincerely,
Velvet

Short and sweet. I rip out the page and fold it into a square, but I don't know what to do with it. And then it hits me—I'll give it to the manager at the bowling alley. Surely he'll see Diamond Jim again. He has to. Mama stops in my doorway, and I close my journal with a quick snap.

"I left some paperwork unfinished at the shop, and I need to run over quick." In the dim light, I see she's grinning and dressed way too nicely for a work errand. And it's a little late.

"OK." Now I know my pep talk worked!

"Velvet …" Mama pauses at the door. "Thank you again for the poem."

I smile. "You're welcome, Mama. I meant every word."

Before I know it, I'm in Mama's room again, determined to get closer to the truth. I open her journal and read the next entry:

I think God gives us warnings about people and their
intentions. You know, a gut feeling. And I believe we
feel the warnings God sends but choose to gamble, hold

all the cards in our own hands, like I did. I heard God whisper the night I met Diamond Jim. I heard him loud and clear, "Lynette, don't go." He whispered it straight to my heart. I shook my head like God was a pesky bug flying around my ear. Looking back, I wish I would have stopped, even just for a moment, and listened. 'Cause he was right. I shouldn't have gone.

Once word got out that I was pregnant and Diamond Jim dumped me because of it, he came back. I guess he didn't want the whole town thinking he was a lousy excuse for a man. So he rolled up in his shiny Cadillac full of pride, telling everyone he knew he was going to be a daddy, acting like his baby was the best thing in the whole world. He said it was time to settle down and plant some roots in Sack City with the love of his life. He said, "I was confused, Lynette, in shock. It took time to get everything clear in my head. But now I'm here for you, for the baby."

I was leery of him, of course, I had to be. He showed up acting like there should have been fanfare and confetti surrounding his big arrival back to reality. But his embarrassment about abandoning me and the baby, and his begging for forgiveness gave me the power. And his recommitment felt good. I started to trust his plans and promises. Lord knows I didn't want to do this alone. So I forgave him and took him back. Pops and Ditty took DJ back too, though they were reluctant about it. They did it for my sake, and the baby's.

DJ said he was ready for the baby, ready to be a

daddy, until a real, live baby girl was right in front of him. Velvet Mary was born on May 1, weighing 7 pounds and 13 ounces. She was 21 inches long with soft brown hair. DJ wasn't there when Velvet was born. He said he had a sales trip. Ditty was by my side when Dr. Dearberg handed my sweet daughter to me, with her eyes wide open and her heart ready to be loved. I whispered in her ear, "You are meant to be here, baby girl."

I begged him not to go, but he said he'd only be a few short hours away. He didn't call to check on me, the love of his life who was about to have his baby any moment, and he had no idea she had arrived until after we were home. She was sleeping peacefully beside me in our bed, and I was studying her face, memorizing the shape of her tiny nose and the lift of her lip while she dreamed, when I heard his car rumble over the rocks in the driveway.

I wasn't sure how I would handle that moment. I was so tired. So I pulled my baby close, braced myself for grace and called on God's strength. DJ tiptoed into the room, and when he saw us snuggled beneath the covers, he fell to his knees beside the bed and put his hand on top of Velvet's soft head.

"Lynette, I'm so sorry," he said and asked if it was a boy or a girl. I introduced him to Velvet Mary, and both of us wept. He rocked on his knees, shaking his head in disbelief, asked if she was healthy and how I was doing. I said she was perfect and then fatigue took my words. My eyes became my voice and as my tears fell, DJ wiped them away, promising to never leave our side. "I'm so

sorry," he said, over and over again. He crawled in bed and held us close.

"Your daddy is here now," I whispered. For the first time in two days, I slept deeply, wrapped in the security of DJ and Velvet.

Velvet's presence, like DJ's, filled a void I didn't know was empty. And for a while, I felt like I was part of something bigger. We were a family. And then he went back to bowling every chance he got, working longer hours selling insurance, traveling for days at a time. It was like he couldn't stand to be with us. When he was home, he was irritable and restless, unable to share a simple meal together without losing his patience. I'd sit across the table from him and watch him shift in his chair and push his meat and potatoes around like a pouting child. Nothing made him happy, not me, not Velvet, and I found myself avoiding him.

I tried to figure it out. Was his job too stressful? Did he have another woman? Was he involved in something dangerous? I couldn't ask him. I couldn't make him talk to me. So I held Velvet close, like my life depended on it. And I begged God to change him.

Mama pulls into the driveway, so I stash the journal, run to my room and get into bed. I hear her whistling a tune I haven't heard before. I close my eyes thinking about my daddy and wondering why he was so restless. When I fall asleep, I dream of Mama and Mr. Sullivan dancing by the gas pump, a romantic rendezvous surrounded by broken-down trucks and worn-out rubber tires. She's looking into his eyes, telling him he's always been the one. It starts to rain lightly, and the raindrops wash away her past.

When I wake up the next morning, there's a note from Mama on the kitchen table telling me she's off to work early and to have a great day. I smile. Then I look at the clock and realize I have time to read. I return to the journal and the next entry:

Velvet was almost 6 months old. It was November, and the weather was changing as quickly as my circumstances. Pops was sick, coughing all the time. Ditty was worried, and so was I. The two of them came over for dinner, and in the middle of our meal, he said, "I don't want to scare anyone, but I stopped breathing today." He said it was only for a few seconds and that his cough was getting worse.

Ditty was furious. "You're going straight to the doctor tomorrow, old man, do you hear me?" she said. She asked Pops if he was trying to scare her to death. He grumbled about how much he hated doctors, but he knew Ditty was serious.

Of course, DJ wasn't there. He never was. He was traveling five or six days a week, leaving me home alone with Velvet and a big empty bed. When he was home, he barely looked at us. I tried my best to hold it all together, but with Pops being sick, I really needed him.

I stop reading and think about Pops. I only remember him being sick. He coughed all the time. Some days he'd have a burst of energy, like he did the day he brought the Virgin Mary statue home. But Ditty always worried about him, and I prayed all the time for the Lord to heal him. I was so young; I was confused why God didn't make him better.

It was the only funeral I ever attended. Mama and Ditty dressed in black, and I wore a little blue dress Ditty sewed for me. As I walked up to the front of the church, I first saw Pops' nose peaking above the side of the casket. He loved to make me giggle with jokes about how big his nose was. His skin was waxy, and his hair looked like it had been brushed for too long. The hairs that had been wild and woolly now sat eerily still on the top of his head.

I watched as Mama and Ditty both broke down. Even at a young age I was protective of them, and though I already missed Pops terribly, I let my grief take a backseat to theirs. Ditty tried to stand taller, to bring forth the strength she needed to say her biggest goodbye. She whispered, "I've loved you my whole life. My whole life." I squeezed her hand tight.

"I'm gonna give him a kiss," she said with a quick glance around the church, like a schoolgirl who could get in trouble. She puckered her lips, bent down, and kissed him.

It was just like all the times before she had leaned in to kiss him at the kitchen table. He'd exaggerate the exchange by puckering his lips and adding a smooching sound for effect. He was always looking to be the center of attention, and there in the casket, in his white button-down shirt, he was.

"They're cold," Ditty said. We all giggled a little, releasing some of our sadness.

Pops was the closest thing to a daddy I ever had. I know it

was hard on him when Mama got her heart broken because it was the one thing he couldn't fix. Ditty told me once that Pops tried to track down Diamond Jim a few times; he wanted him to know about the beautiful daughter he left behind.

I crisscross my legs, close my eyes, and whisper, "Hi, Pops." I get back to the journal:

As Velvet got bigger, she needed more and more attention. She was crawling with one arm across the living room carpet. Her little knees were always red and irritated, so I rubbed Vaseline on them to keep them from drying out. She didn't know about my worry or pain surrounding Diamond Jim, and I didn't let her see it. Her sweet eyes always showed promise and hope.

One night I was startled awake like I'd had a nightmare. My heart raced, and my hands were on the bed, feeling my way back to reality. The clock read 4:45 a.m., and I realized DJ wasn't next to me. His dirty underwear was still lying on the floor where he'd taken them off. I looked in the bathroom and then the living room. He wasn't there. I went to the kitchen, and there was no sign of him. Did he have a work trip I'd forgotten? I looked for a note. There wasn't one. I opened the front door, stepped barefoot onto the front steps, and looked for his Cadillac. The crisp November morning air took my breath away, and all I saw was gravel where his car used to be. He was gone.

I went back to the bedroom and opened his dresser. There were no crisp folded blue jeans, no clean white

T-shirts, no rolled socks, just empty drawers. Near the front door, in the closet, there was no suitcase, just a clump of dust bunnies where it had been. I slid down to the floor and wailed, pressing my hands over my mouth to muffle the sounds. I looked up at the ceiling, searching for God, but he was nowhere to be found. I was alone, abandoned. The restless man I loved couldn't do the right thing, wouldn't do the right thing. I shouldn't have been surprised, but I was.

My eyes begin to water. *Lord, why? Why do people make terrible decisions that hurt people?*

CHAPTER 24
LOST AND FOUND

D iamond Jim left Mama and me all alone. I suddenly feel a sense of urgency, like if I waste another minute, I'll miss my chance. I have to get my note to the Strike Zone. I throw on my slippers and run to the tree. Mercy stands under it, squinting in my direction.

"Is it pajama day?" she asks.

"No, I'm not going to school today, Mercy. I'm skipping."

"Velvet?"

"Don't worry, I'll update you after school. I have to find my daddy. I have to!"

Mercy looks at me with understanding but also concern.

"I wrote him back. I'm gonna find him."

"Do you want my help?"

"No, but thank you. I wouldn't want to get you in any trouble. Besides, I think I need to do this on my own. And there's so much more to read in the journal, I have to see it through to the end."

"Are you sure about this, Velvet?"

"Yes."

Mercy looks at her wristwatch. "OK, good luck. I'll stop by right after school."

I run back to the house, pick up the phone and dial the shop. Mama has been especially cheery, despite the fact that just days ago she stood in the yard with a shotgun, ready to shoot Diamond Jim. I still think it's Mr. Sullivan that's putting a spring in her step or, as Mama would say, a "click in my heels."

I don't think Mama and Mr. Sullivan are officially dating. Still, I do think Diamond Jim leaving a note for me without contacting Mama may have sent the message once and for all that he doesn't have the courage to face her.

"Sullivan's Auto Body. This is Lynette speaking. How may I help you?"

"Mama, it's me. If it's OK with you, I'm gonna stay home from school today. My wrist is aching, and I feel like I need to rest a bit."

The lie, like a silver pinball, shoots off my tongue straight into the phone.

Mama pauses on the other end. "Do you need to see a doctor?"

"No. I need a day to rest and keep my arm propped up on a pillow."

I wait for her response.

"OK, I'll call the school nurse and let her know."

Phew. I look out the kitchen window. *Lord, I know lying shouldn't be this easy, but it is, and I'm sorry.*

"Thanks, Mama."

I hang up the phone, walk to my room and find my note to Diamond Jim. I can do this. I can find him. I rummage through the junk drawer to find an envelope and put the note inside. I write on the front of it, "To Diamond Jim, the Strike Zone Champ." I put the envelope on the kitchen table. Now I have to wait until 10 a.m. for the bowling alley to open.

I crawl back into Mama's unmade bed and grab her journal. There's a pen wedged between two pages toward the back. A newer entry reads:

What am I waiting for? For DJ to come back and walk through the front door? He was here, goddammit. He was right here! Instead of knocking on the door, he came in the middle of the night, like the coward he is, and left a note on Velvet's window. My sweet girl broke her wrist trying to reach for it. I've searched the roads for him, up and down. I've even stalked his old stomping grounds, the Strike Zone and the Hickory. I'm like a roaring lion, unafraid, intentional, searching and waiting for him to show up. If and when he does, I'll be ready with Pops' rifle. I won't need a permit or permission. As far as I'm concerned, it'll be hunting season. He won't see me coming, but he sure will feel me when I get there.

My mouth drops open and I realize I'm shivering under the sheets. Mama wants to kill Diamond Jim. I wonder if Ditty hid Pops' shotgun. I go out to the shed to look for it.

I was 12 when Pops taught me how to use the gun. He said, "Velvet, it's time to do some shooting." He took me down past the railroad tracks and into the woods. He lined up five wooden duck decoys on an old fence. He explained the parts of the gun and how it works. He showed me how to handle it when it's not being used, and then he showed me how to use it.

First he did it. "Steady your arm like this," he said. "And then you pull the trigger like this." Hearing that first shot made me jump out of my skin. Then Pops put the gun in my hands and stood behind me, holding my arms in position. One, two, three, we pulled the trigger together. Sensing my nervousness, Pops said, "Come on now, you ain't gonna get good at something unless you keep at it."

I got used to the sound and the kickback after a few more shots. We stayed out there for hours until I finally shot a decoy straight off the fence. Pops said, "Your mama isn't gonna believe this!"

I look around the old shed, its contents now covered in cobwebs. Pops has been gone for years, but I can still hear his voice. I miss him so much. I see the shotgun. Ditty probably thinks she hid it well—it's tucked in beside an old wooden cupboard—but it's still visible. I hide it behind the cupboard so it's completely out of sight. I lean the rake and shovel against the cupboard.

I head back inside to Mama's bed and glance at the clock. The Strike Zone will open soon. I pick up reading where I left off:

He's been gone for so long now. Not a word from anyone about his whereabouts. It's like he died. Sometimes I wish he had. But something inside me tells me he's alive, rolling around in his Cadillac, pretending life is grand, and it makes me sick to my stomach.

When Velvet learned to walk, she'd wake with the sun and stand next to my bed, just waiting for me to move. I'd open my eyes to an angel with her sweet face and sleepy waves. She'd caress my cheek with her little hand and say, "Mama, the sun is up." She stood like her daddy, with her heels in and her toes out. I would try to set her toes straight, determined she wouldn't be like him, but they popped back out every time. She has her daddy's charm, too, and it's what pulls me from the bed I want to stay in all day, leading me to the brightness of the living room, out the front door and into the world. I thank God for Velvet every day because without her I'd be drowning in a bed of tears.

The clock reads 9:30 a.m. I put the journal back and close the drawer on Mama's past like I've done so many times. I think about Mama falling asleep next to this nightstand and its drawer filled with her pain, and it makes me want to throw the whole thing out. The garbage man could pick it up on Monday with the rest of the trash in Sack City, and Mama could get a new one with clean, empty drawers full of potential.

I brush my teeth, comb my hair and put on the outfit I would have worn to school. I look at my cast. My wrist still aches, and I wonder what people in town will say when they notice I'm not at school.

I look at the envelope with Diamond Jim's name on it and second guess my plan. I grab it quickly, before I decide that he's not worth it and that the past doesn't matter anymore and head out the door. The spring air is surprisingly warm, like summer decided to borrow a day, and the flags at the top of Tender Vine Lane are aflutter. I round the corner and head into town.

The Strike Zone looks different in the morning. The neon lights aren't nearly as bright, and the parking lot is empty except for one white car. I look down at the envelope and realize my sweaty hand has made the writing—his name—bleed onto my skin. I try to rub it off, but it stays put. I open the door with my good hand and squint as I adjust to the darkness. The bowling alley is quiet except for the beeping and binging of arcade games begging to be played, and I feel like I shouldn't be here. I walk toward the counter where the lanes and shoes are rented.

"Can I help you?"

I jump at the voice emerging from the silence.

"Yes. Sorry," I say. "You startled me."

The manager doesn't apologize. Instead, he stares hard at me. He probably thinks I've misplaced something and hopes to send me to the lost-and-found bin so he can get back to whatever it is he's doing. If only it was that easy. If only everything we've lost could be found in a bin.

"I was wondering if you've seen Diamond Jim around?" I try to sound casual, but my voice cracks.

The manager raises an eyebrow.

"You know …" I point down the hall. "The Strike Zone Champ?"

I avoid his gaze while I wait for an answer.

"Yeah, I've seen him. He's in town, visiting a friend."

Yes! He he's still here. Am I the friend?

"Can you tell me when he usually bowls …" I read the

name badge attached to his short-sleeved maroon bowling shirt, "Bill?"

Bill grabs a rag and starts polishing a pair of shoes from the size eight cubby. "He doesn't usually stay long ..." He pauses and sets down the shoe. "He may be gone by now."

I look down at the carpet, so he won't see the disappointment on my face. Bill clears his throat.

"But when he is around, he usually comes midmorning." This declaration of hope lifts my eyes to his. "He likes to bowl alone," he says.

I glance at the clock above Bill's head. It's 10:22. Something in my gut sparks to life, and I know he's coming today. Mama always says trust my gut; she says the body doesn't lie, and I believe her.

I pull out the note and hand it to Bill. "Can you give him this ... when he comes?"

Bill takes the note and says, "OK."

I turn to leave, and for the first time I don't go down the Strike Zone Champ hallway, like the little girl who never met her daddy did. I don't need to stare at a picture of his face anymore. Soon I'll see the real thing.

I sit and wait at the park across the street, the one where Bobby kissed me. No one is there; it's as empty as the Strike Zone parking lot. All the kids are in school, and the air is starting to change, the way it does before a storm blows through town. I swing the way I did with Bobby, one elbow around one chain and my good hand around the other. I push off with my legs until I'm creating my own wind, my own joy. Swinging alone reminds me of the time when God himself visited me and spoke in a summer whisper as clear as the church bells on Sunday morning. I smile and get lost in the breeze, forgetting about the letter. I stretch my face toward the sky, searching for the Holy Spirit.

The energy changes, and the wind stops blowing. I stop pumping my legs. The swing keeps moving but sways slower and slower. My body feels heavy, like a brick being tossed back and forth. I'm afraid my heart might stop. A black Cadillac pulls into the Strike Zone parking lot.

It glides into a spot near the entrance, and I wait for him, holding my breath. It has to be him. The air is so still I can hear the door creak when he finally pops it open. The swing stops, and I sit, suspended in the air, legs dangling like wet noodles. I try to hide my face behind the chain I'm holding, that's holding me. I wait to see my daddy for the first time.

He slides his legs out, his boots hit the ground, and he stands and straightens his shirt. He's taller than I thought he'd be, and even from here, I can tell he's handsome. His face is rugged but warm. He runs a hand through his dark hair and looks up at the sky. I notice his stance—Mama was right, it's just like mine. Then he opens the back car door, and I see the red velvet interior that was the "damn near softest thing" Mama's ever felt. He pulls out a black bowling bag with a red monogram. I'm pretty sure it reads, "DJ." I gasp like the car itself wasn't enough proof.

He walks to the entrance, and once his back is to me, I hop off the swing and pace. Should I go in now? In a minute Bill will hand him my note. He'll either open it right there or put it in his pocket, too cool to read it in front of the manager. When he does read it, will it make him smile? I plant my feet. I realize it doesn't matter if he reads my note at all. I'm here. He's there.

I walk, determined, down the hill to the Strike Zone to finally meet its champ.

In the parking lot, I'm pulled like a magnet to the Cadillac. My courage rises and falls like I'm on a ride at the state fair. One second, I'm 16, fierce and brave, and the next, I'm the little girl he left behind. It's the little girl who stands here staring at his car. I put my hand on the Cadillac emblem, as if touching it is the only way to make it real. Mama said Diamond Jim's car was classy and alluring, but to me it looks rough around the edges, worn out. I guess things can't stay shiny and new forever. If his car says anything about him, I think Diamond Jim is tired, too. I'll bet he's no longer the flashy man who lured Mama with his charm and his possessions.

I peek in the car window and see the red velvet interior is also shabby. Something catches my eye—the shimmering black rosary beads Mama said "swayed from side to side" as she and my daddy drove down a moonlit country road. *God, what will I say to him?*

I touch the door and realize besides the note he taped to my bedroom window, this car is the closest I've ever been to my daddy since he left Mama and me. It feels strangely familiar, like it was mine a long time ago. Standing next to it makes my stomach twist, and my hands shake so badly I want to run back up the hill and hide. Or go home, back to Tender Vine Lane, to Mama. Or, instead of hiding, I could go straight to Sullivan's Auto Body and tell Mama he's here, just a few blocks away. We could both confront him at the bowling alley. A sneak attack of the Underwood women. He wouldn't know what hit him.

I look up at the dark clouds rolling in. A storm is definitely coming. *Lord, I need you. I'm about to meet the daddy you chose for me. You have us both here, so help me. Show me why.* With all the 16-year-old courage I can muster, I take a deep breath as I walk up and open the door.

As far as I know, there are three people here—Bill, Diamond Jim and me. My eyes search the lanes until I see his back. He's in lane six. He's right there. And already bowling. The Strike Zone Champ bowls a spare, leaving one pin standing. He shakes his head in disappointment. The jukebox is playing, but I can't concentrate on what song it is. My daddy is standing 20 feet away. He turns and waits at the ball return, and then he sees me. He pauses and raises one hand in greeting, a white flag tossed into the air.

He keeps his hand up a little longer as I walk toward him. His ball shoots up and spins in the return. He doesn't touch it; he waits for me. But I'm stuck. I can't take the last few steps. It's like the floor is made of rubber cement.

"Is that you, Velvet?"

He squints. I've never heard him say my name before. It stirs up tears I don't want him to see.

"Velvet?" He says it again.

"Yes," I say. "It's me."

My chin quivers as I try hard not to cry. I wait for what will happen next. Will he hug me? Pick me up? Tell me how sorry he is?

None of those things happen. Instead, Diamond Jim strolls right past me. I smell the hard work and pine Mama so loved. He says something to Bill at the counter and comes back with a pair of shoes and a shiny purple bowling ball.

"Can you bowl?" he asks.

I wipe the tears from my eyes, like I've been challenged to fight. "Yes," I sputter. "I can."

"Well, let's see what you got!"

He gives me a grin, and it calms my nerves and breaks my heart all at once. I know it's the same smile that made Mama weak in the knees, the one that lured her into his backseat and onto that soft velvet. It's the grin that sparked joy, ignited a flame, and ultimately, wrecked her for life.

I take a seat at lane six and untie my shoes. It all feels like a dream, like the Strike Zone is an imaginary place. Diamond Jim fumbles with the scorecard, and I watch intently as he writes my name in pencil at the top of it. I've been with him for only a few minutes, but he already feels like the good kind of trouble, like the sneaking-into-a-movie-theater-through-the-back-door kind. I can tell he's one of those guys who can get you so caught up in a moment that you don't even think about the problems it may cause later. For the first time ever, I understand why Mama lost herself in him. Guilt creeps in as I make the final loop in my laces. How will I tell her about this? What if she comes looking for me, for him? Will this break her heart forever?

"What happened to your wrist?" Diamond Jim asks, frowning

"It's a long story."

"That's good to hear," he says. "My story's a long one too."

His smile matches his eyes now, tender. I notice the lines around his face that don't exist in the picture down the hall. I can see how sorry he is. We look directly at each other, and the reasons he left and the time I've spent without him don't seem so fragile anymore. The story is just that—a story of something that happened a long time ago. And though I'm ready to hear it, I'm also ready to just be with him, my daddy, right here in lane six, with Bill the manager shining shoes at the counter, and a song I don't know the words to floating in the air.

CHAPTER 25
KEGLER

We bowl for hours, sometimes talking and sometimes not. I could ask him the hard questions, like why or how. I could tell him I never got the birthday cards he sent throughout the years, that Mama hid them to punish him, but the rhythm of the game takes over and I let myself go, led by the Strike Zone Champ. He says things like, "You gotta belly the ball," and, "Change the position of your hand," his skin making contact with mine. Or "Try to keep your chicken wing down" when my elbow lifts too far from my body during wind up. When I leave a few pins in the alley, he chuckles, "Looks like you left some of Grandma's teeth standing."

His bowling lingo is a whole other language, and as he speaks it, I can tell he really wants me to know it. I do too, I want to know it all.

"You're gonna be a great kegler," he says.

"A kegler?"

"A bowler," he explains, grinning.

I smile back looking into his eyes, the ones I thought I knew so well from studying his picture for so many years. Right here in front me, his eyes are different. There's so much more to see.

He doesn't hold my gaze long. He keeps teaching me, one frame at a time.

"Now, let the ball go, nice and easy." I want it to be easy, to release the ball effortlessly, but my grip is tense and I'm still holding it too tight.

I look at the clock above the arcade sign. "I better be going."

I don't tell him why, but I need to be back before Mama gets home so I can figure out what to tell her about my day.

"I understand," he says, and he pauses. "I was planning on leaving today. You know, getting back on the road."

He averts his eyes, takes out a blue rag and shines his glittery black bowling ball. I don't know how to respond. His leaving again cuts at my heart, and the hours we've spent together seem like they never happened.

"I left my score book here and stopped in to grab it. That's when Bill handed me your note." He pulls it from his back pocket. "I was hoping I'd see you, Velvet."

My chin starts to tremble again, and my abandoned words push past one another like preschoolers elbowing and shoving, trying to get to the front of the line. I realize I may never see him again; this might be my only chance to know his truth.

I take a deep breath. "How come it took you so long to show up? You could have seen me all this time, but you didn't even try. You weren't even brave enough to hand me your note in person." I hold up my cast. "You want to know what happened to my wrist? You! I was stretching my arm for your note, and I fell. I crashed to the ground, reaching for you." Tears cascade down my cheeks, and I don't try to stop them.

He puts the ball down and stuffs the rag into the side of his bag.

"I tried," he says. "I sent you birthday cards every year. I had a feeling Lynette wasn't giving them to you. I decided, since you're older now, I'd try to get a message to you myself."

He puts his hands in his pockets and nods toward my cast. "Looks like I messed that up, too."

My shoulders release some of the weight I've held all these years—the feeling of being left behind, the burden of Mama's pain. He tried.

It's Diamond Jim's turn to cry. His tears well up like they're collecting inside a leaky faucet.

"Velvet, I sat outside your home many a night when I passed through town."

The sound of my name coming out of his mouth again catches me off guard.

"Why didn't you come to the door?"

He clears his throat and tugs at the hem of his shirt. "I didn't wanna hurt your Mama anymore."

He sits down and pulls a handkerchief out of his pocket.

"I've read Mama's journal," I confess, unashamed. "You left her all alone."

Diamond Jim hangs his head. "I wasn't good enough for her." And there, in the middle of the Strike Zone, is his truth. "I tried to be, but something in me was always unsettled." He dabs his tears.

I picture the confident man Mama fell head over heels for, but it all seems lost now that I see what he thought he was to

Mama and me—unworthy of our love. His truth no longer left a gaping hole in our relationship but mended it instead.

"I've watched her sleep through her window ..." His voice trails. "I wanted to walk through the front door like I used to, lay beside her and hold her tight, tell her I was sorry I couldn't be the man she needed me to be for her," he inhales deeply and exhales, "and for you."

He reaches for my hand, and I squeeze it. I think of what Father Matthew said about Jesus sitting with the sinners, the tax collectors and the adulterers, while others looked on in shock. Jesus didn't care about the decisions they'd made, he only cared they were sitting there with him.

"It's gonna be OK," I say and call on God to let it be so. *Lord, thank you for this.* I squeeze Diamond Jim's hand again. "I have to go. Mama will wonder where I am."

He stands and opens his arms, and we hug like I've always wanted to.

"I hope one day, instead of standing outside in the dark, you'll come to the front door and knock."

He smiles and nods yes. "You're a sweet girl, Velvet. Just like your mama."

I leave the daddy I never knew, thankful he's no longer a face behind a picture frame. I step outside expecting it to be bright, but it's eerily dark and still, like the wind is playing hide-and-seek and afraid to breathe for fear of being found. Thunder rumbles in the distance. I wonder if I should go back in ask Diamond Jim for a ride. I come to my senses quickly. What would Mama do if she saw me roll up in Diamond Jim's Cadillac? I pray I have time to make it home before the storm and run toward our house on Tender Vine Lane, to Mama.

Residents of Sack City are closing their windows and locking their gates. What started as a beautiful sunny day has completely turned, and I can't keep my eyes off the sky. As I get closer to home, Bobby's grandma spots me and hollers from her front door, "Velvet, you better get inside quick! This is gonna be some kind of storm!"

I stop for a second and stand under the strength of the old weeping willow, its wispy dipping branches resting silently on the grass. The flags that whipped against the wind earlier hang motionless against the poles. Mrs. Johnson slams her door shut tightly. I think about spending a minute with Mary, telling her about my day and how my heart has grown bigger in just a few hours.

Mama interrupts my thoughts, shouting from her truck window as she pulls in the driveway. "Velvet, are you trying to get yourself killed? What in the hell are you doing out here? Get inside this very second!"

She hurries out of the truck and to the front door while she nervously scans the sky. "Lord, have mercy!"

The sky exhales a blast of air, making it impossible for me to get to Mary. A bolt of lightning flashes above, like it's looking for a fight.

"Velvet!" Mama screams.

I try running to her, but another gust of wind comes and knocks my butt to the ground. Mama shrieks and holds tight to the door, which looks like it's about to blow off its hinges. There's a rustle in the bushes—it's Mrs. Johnson's cat, Mr. Jenkins. He's staring at me. As another shock of lighting illuminates the sky, Mama barks, "Velvet, goddammit, get in this house already before we all blow away!"

I don't have time to apologize to God for her swearing. Instead, I reach out to grab Mr. Jenkins, but he scurries away. I push myself forward while the roaring wind tries to carry me sideways. Mama has both hands on the doorknob now, and I climb up the front steps, my hands gripping the metal railing. My hair feels like it could blow right off my head, but I make it inside and Mama shuts the door. I go straight to the kitchen window to get a good look at what's coming and see Mrs. Johnson's patio furniture tumbling down the street.

"Velvet, get away from the window! Don't they teach you nothin' during those storm drills at school?" Mama moves fast around the house, gathering candles and matches. Then she runs to the phone and calls Ditty. "Where are you?" she shouts through the receiver. "You stay put, you hear?"

"Mama, is a tornado coming?" I ask when she hangs up the phone.

"I don't know, but the town will sound a siren for us to take cover."

Outside, the branches of the willow are in full swing, dancing in the dark. The garden vines twist up to the clouds and tangle into each other.

"Let's go!" Mama says.

"Where?"

"The bathtub!"

There's one window in the bathroom, and Mama tacks a towel over it. As she finishes, the power goes out with a bang.

She lights candles along the bathroom sink, and the flickering flames throw skipping shadows against the pink tiles. We get into the empty tub. I wrap my arms tightly around Mama, snuggle in, and wait. I could tell her right now that I met my daddy today, but I don't. She starts to hum a hymn I've heard a million times, and I join in.

The lightning flashes through the gaps where the towel doesn't reach the window frame. I look at the ceiling, wondering if the roof will hold. The rain isn't gently falling—it's beating down like a prizefighter throwing punch after punch, challenging our little trailer to plant its feet and hold steady. I pray we don't end up like one of those trailer parks ravaged by tornadoes on the news, with roofs caved in and everyone's lives exposed.

"I'm scared, Mama!"

"Ditty always says, 'God's gonna take you when God's gonna take you,'" Mama says, pulling me in even closer. "But he ain't taking us today, Velvet."

The rain slows to spits and sputters, and so does the wind. God opened a bottle, and then put a cork in it. The lightning continues, but it's in the distance now, wavy sketches of electricity in the far-off sky. Mama and I, feeling safe enough to move, climb out of the tub together and she goes to the front door.

"We got lucky, Velvet. It was only a severe thunderstorm." Then she asks, "Where were you coming from, anyway?"

Instead of answering, I go back to the bathroom, grab a few candles, and bring them to the living room. Mama opens the front door, and Mr. Jenkins races in and scurries straight under our couch. Mama shrieks. "What in the goddamn hell?"

I laugh so hard, I nearly drop the candles. "It's Mr. Jenkins. He must be scared from the storm. He won't hurt anybody. I'll take him back over to Mrs. Johnson's in a little bit, after he calms down." *Sorry Lord, for Mama's swearing.*

The cat has Mama forgetting her question, which is fine by me. I'm not ready to tell her yet. We look out at the mess in the front yard. Mrs. Johnson's patio furniture cushions are scattered near Mary, and two of her chairs lie across the street at the entrance to the trailer park. The whole park is filled with leaves, twigs and branches. The storm snapped up Mama's garden gate, leaving it hanging loose on its hinges.

It's interesting how God gives us warnings before a storm, like he did today by hiding the wind. I wonder what kind of warning I can give Mama about my visit with Diamond Jim so she can brace for it. Did it even happen? I look at my hand that held his and remind myself it did happen.

"Woo-wee," Mama says, shaking her head. "That was some kind of storm."

She walks out to the garden and tries to push the old gate into place. When she realizes it will take more than her own strength to get it back in position, she picks up a few branches and sticks instead. As I watch her, I wonder what her reaction will be when I tell her about what happened today.

Mama comes back inside and looks for more candles while I try to lure Mr. Jenkins out from under the couch. When Mama says, "The power might be out for a few days, Velvet," I imagine confessing in the dark of our living room that I spent my day with my daddy at the Strike Zone.

"I love nights like this," Mama says. "You know, when you get to just—be."

I know what she means. Not having any electricity feels different, like camping but with the comfort of our own beds and a flushing toilet. As I'm agreeing with Mama, there's a knock at the door. I gasp out loud and cover my mouth with my good hand. Diamond Jim! It's happening! He's finally here! Now I won't have to tell Mama about my day, he'll say it all. He'll tell her why he was so afraid to love us.

"Lordy, Velvet, it's like you've never heard someone knock on the door before."

I get a hold of Mr. Jenkins and clutch him firmly as Mama walks to the door holding a lilac-scented candle. Mr. Jenkins squeals, wanting to be let down. I hold him tighter.

"Mama, wait!" I say. It's happening. Now! It has to be him!

"What on earth?" Mama says grabbing the doorknob. "Velvet, what has gotten into you?"

What can I say? There's no way to prepare her for what's behind the door. She opens it and air rushes in, bringing with it the fresh smell of rain. I stand behind Mama and peer over her shoulder, excited to see Diamond Jim again. Only it's not him. It's not even Mrs. Johnson, looking for her cat. Instead, standing at our door is Mama's redheaded nemesis, pink-faced and teary-eyed. Why is Mrs. Evans crying on our front steps?

Mama takes a step back in shock, then sucks in her belly and puffs up her chest. "What do you want?"

Mrs. Evans cries harder, dabbing at her eyes with a hanky and choking on her words.

"Spit it out already! What is it?" Mama demands.

Mrs. Evans blots her mascara before it drips onto our front step. "I came to tell you … Diamond Jim …" She lets out a wail. "He's … dead."

Dead? I drop Mr. Jenkins and he runs wildly out the door. Mama stands motionless, staring at Mrs. Evans.

"I thought y'all should know," she says, pushing her hair out of her face. "Do you hear me, Lynette?"

Mama lets go of the doorknob and kicks the door closed, her hands balled up by her sides. I push my way past Mama and open the door. Mrs. Evans is halfway down the steps.

"What happened to him?" I demand. "I was just with him! He can't be dead!"

I hear the words come out of my mouth, but I don't believe them.

Mrs. Evans turns to look at me, her eyes soft and concerned. She reaches out her hand to touch my shoulder.

"I'm so sorry to tell you this, Velvet, but your daddy was struck by lightning while helping an elderly couple get their windows closed up during the storm. The paramedics said he didn't feel a thing. He died instantly. I'm so sorry." Mrs. Evans continues to hold my shoulder. "About everything," she says.

I picture my daddy, the Strike Zone Champ, in his bowling clothes, running from his car to help the old folks. They were probably so grateful to have a kind, strong man to help them stay safe. My heart stabs with a pain that has no limit. A few hours ago, we were together in lane six, with the music and the lights.

"I thought y'all should know," Mrs. Evans says again.

I can tell her intentions are good. She's trying to be kind and do the right thing.

"Your mama's gonna need you, Velvet," she adds.

Mama? What about me? "OK." I say.

As Mrs. Evans turns to go, stray raindrops fall from a nearby tree and land on my arm. The storm has changed nothing and everything. He's dead. My daddy is dead. I turn to see Mama standing in the doorway, stuck in place. Her eyes are foggy. Her fists are still clenched and ready to fight for him. I lost the daddy I had just met. *Lord, don't let me lose Mama too.*

"Mama?" I guide her to the couch. I sit close to her, our legs touching, and put her hand in mine. "It's gonna be all right, Mama."

Is it? The words feel flat, empty. I said the same thing to Diamond Jim, and now he's gone. Where do we go from here? He's never coming back, and Mama is far away, lost behind those eyes.

Ditty comes bursting through the door, and she can tell we've already heard the shocking news. She tries to get through to Mama, waving her hands in front of her face, putting a glass of water to her lips, calling out her name. But nothing works.

"Should we call the doctor, Ditty?"

"No, honey. I'm afraid they don't have medicine for this." Ditty reaches out to console me, but I run to my room and pull my pillow over my face. I hear Ditty calling out to me. "Velvet, it's gonna be all right."

I know it isn't true. Nothing is ever going to be the same. I scream into my pillow. The storm lasted a mere 12 minutes, and though it didn't cause much external damage, the news about my daddy feels like it blew the roof off our home, leaving us exposed and crumpled.

While I cry in my room, Mama sits motionless on the couch for hours. I hear Ditty try every trick in the book. When I finally come back to the living room to check on Mama, she rises from the couch, candles flickering all around her. Ditty and I follow her to her room.

"Lynette?" Ditty says.

"Mama, are you OK?"

She doesn't say a word. She enters the bathroom, and Ditty tries to go in with her, but Mama pushes the door shut before she can slip through. We put our ear to the door and hear Mama peeing. It makes me feel better, like her heart might be shut down, but there's a part of her that's still working. *Thank you, Lord.* We listen to Mama wash her hands like normal, and then she comes out and walks into her room.

"It's horrible what happened to him, Mama. I can't believe it." I choke back tears.

Mama takes her clothes off and stands naked in front of us. She pulls the covers back and crawls into her bed. Ditty goes straight to her, tugging the blankets up and over her skin. I carry a candle to her bedside and kiss her on the forehead. Has she forgotten that we're a team?

"Mama, you need to talk to me." Panic makes my voice shaky, and Ditty holds my shoulders to steady me. "Mama, we both lost him. He loved us both. He told me!"

Mama finally looks into my eyes.

"I met him, Mama."

Mama blinks a few times.

"Velvet?" Ditty asks.

"It's true." I look at Ditty. "I met him earlier today. We

bowled for hours together, and he told me he was sorry. He cried. He said he never felt like he was worthy of our love. That's why he left. He couldn't bear to fail us by staying, so he left, thinking it'd be better for us both."

Mama blinks again, and a tear rolls down her cheek.

"He stopped by the house all the time, in the wee hours of the night. He told me he stood outside your window and watched you sleep. He wanted to crawl in bed beside you and hold you, but he couldn't. He was afraid he would hurt you more than he already did. He was broken, Mama."

She sits up and the sheets fall, exposing her naked breasts. She makes the first sound she's made since Mrs. Evans came to the door, a yelp of pain that tortures my heart. Her hands still in fists, she beats at the mattress while her tears fall onto her chest. She keeps howling until there's nothing left but heaving. I kiss her salty, wet cheeks to remind her she is loved. She is love. I reach for her hand, and she squeezes mine back. *Thank you, Lord.*

Then, with a long, deep exhalation, Mama's whole body releases. Still holding my hand, she looks out at the garden. The weeds, now bathed in raindrops, glisten under the light of the moon.

"It's going to be OK, Mama."

She squeezes my hand again and closes her eyes. Ditty covers her bare skin and kisses her forehead. I blow out the candle on the nightstand.

Mama stays in her room for days, getting up only to use the bathroom. She doesn't speak. Like a deer that's been struck by a car, she moves only her eyes like she's begging us to shoot her and take her pain away. I didn't know love could do that, take away your voice. But Mama is proof a broken heart can lock your words far, far away.

Every day, the phone rings off the hook, and Ditty writes down the names of Mama's dancer friends, all wanting to know how Mama is getting on. Funny thing is, every time Ditty hangs up the phone, I hear her say, "Please do keep Lynette in your prayers." Ditty has never shown any interest in prayer or taking time out for God, and her sweet request makes me smile.

Visitors like Mercy and her mama, Mrs. Johnson, and Mrs. Willows sit in our living room, showing their condolences in the form of Bundt cakes and casseroles. Mrs. Evans even drops off Mama's favorite, pecan pie, reminding me that something terrible happened—Diamond Jim died—and it wasn't an awful dream. Meanwhile, Mama is oblivious to the outpouring of kindness beyond her bedroom door.

Mr. Sullivan stops by and stands nervously at the front door with his hands in his front pockets. Eventually, he pulls out a card with "Lynette" written in cursive.

"I'm real sorry about your loss, Velvet," he says.

"Me too. And thank you, Mr. Sullivan."

Although I try to be strong for Mama, I hide away in my room, too, crying and nursing my grieving heart. When I need her to, Ditty listens intently as I tell her about the hours Diamond Jim and I spent together bowling—it's like unless I share every little detail, it wasn't real. I remind myself I met him, I consoled him, I even hugged him. I stare at the smudge on my window where he taped the note and wish I could make time go backwards.

The memory of Mama opening the door to Mrs. Evans

appears often like a terrible recurring dream. I hear Mrs. Evans' words over and over—dead, gone, died. *Lord, I don't understand. And if I try to figure it out, I may go crazy. I'm so sad, but also thankful for the time I had with him and grateful to share his words with Mama. I know you have a plan. A mighty plan. Please make a new path for us. Please.*

CHAPTER 26

AMAZING GRACE

It's been four days since Mrs. Evans showed up on our doorstep with the news about Diamond Jim. The phone rings, Ditty answers and taps on my door.

"Velvet, Mercy is on the line for you." I rub the sleep out of my eyes and push back the covers, wavering about planting my feet in reality. Ditty pauses in my doorway, looks into Mama's room and motions for me to come see. I hustle beside her and watch Mama sitting in bed, writing in her journal, gripping the pen like her life depends on it. Ditty clears her throat to get Mama's attention, but she doesn't look up. She's lost in her words.

"Hello, Mercy?" I want to tell her everything. I need her.

"How are you holding up, Velvet? How's your mama? What can I do to help?"

Mercy asks so many kind questions, I try to answer them in order, but I hear Mama coming down the hall. I look at Ditty and we both stand still, like if we move an inch, she'll head straight back to her room.

"Velvet?" Mercy patiently waits.

"Sorry, I gotta go."

I hang up the phone as Ditty cautiously pulls out a chair for Mama. She is, surprisingly, dressed in her old gardening clothes: faded blue denim overalls with quilted patches of floral fabric Ditty sewed over all the holes.

"I'm not eating," she says, like she knew Ditty would ask. "I've got too much work to do."

She heads to the closet by the front door, and I turn in my seat to get a better look at her. She's rummaging through it in a mad rush. Ditty and I exchange glances, and I shrug my shoulders. I can't put my finger on Mama's mood, but I can tell she's not the same woman we tucked into bed a few days ago. She seems calm and focused.

"Mama, can I help you look for something?" I ask.

"Where in the hell are my green garden boots?"

"I know where they are!" I say, remembering I'd seen them in the shed out back. "I'll go get them!"

I run to the shed in my bare feet like a doctor with a heart on the line. The air and sun remind me it's a new day. I look at the sky and smile, holy goose bumps covering my arms and legs. I trip over a few of Pops' things in the shed, and then I see them; the sun beams a dusty ray of light on Mama's boots. *Thank you, Lord.* I run back in, waving the boots over my head.

"I found them! Do you need help getting them on?"

"Velvet, do I look like I need help putting on my shoes? Child, you remember I danced for a living in costumes that sometimes required me to wear cheap plastic boots two sizes too small. If I could get those on, I think I can get these crusty ol' mudslingers on."

Ditty and I try to hide our smiles. She's back to her old self, her "no one can hold Lynette Underwood down" self. She sits on the chair by the front door and slips on one boot at a time.

"And just what are you planning on doing, Lynette?"

Mama takes her time answering Ditty and looks out the window toward the side yard.

"It's time for me to clean up the garden."

I hold my breath.

"I think you should have some breakfast, or at least a piece of fruit," Ditty says. "You have to take care of yourself. These past few days have been hard on you."

Mama closes her eyes, remembering, and I worry she'll get lost again.

"I'm fine," she says. She stands up and grabs the door handle, and Ditty and I watch her hold it like it's the heaviest door she's ever opened.

"Mama, are you sure you don't want help?"

"No, honey. I need to do this on my own."

Mama walks outside to the garden. Ditty and I shuffle to the kitchen window like two girls spying on their big sister. We watch Mama pull the rusty latch on the garden gate. Because it no longer swings, she lifts it up and away and grimaces at its weight. It's all different shades of green and brown from weather and weeds growing into it for so many years. Plus, the storm jacked it up pretty good. With her green gardening boots, Mama kicks away the weeds and branches, making a path to the middle of the garden.

This is one of those moments, the kind only God can make. Mama is standing in the middle of those weeds with the sun shining right on top of her. Surrounded by a heap of neglect, she stands full of life, like a bud bursting through the earth and reaching for the sun. My mama, a beautiful flower in the middle of a mess. My heart leaps with joy. *Thank you, Lord. Thank you, thank you, thank you!*

"I think she's back, Ditty." I smile and squeeze her hand.

Ditty begins organizing things in the kitchen so she can keep an eye on Mama from the window. Every few minutes she stops in her tracks and says, "I cannot believe my eyes. Velvet, why don't you go out there and see if your mama needs any help?"

"I tried. She says maybe tomorrow she'll need a little help."

I love the word "tomorrow."

With Ditty preoccupied in the kitchen, I sneak into Mama's room and read her latest journal entry:

It's been a long time since I started my morning in prayer, and it's been longer since I've read the Lord's word. This morning, the darkness finally loosened its grip, and I was able to catch a breath. A quick gulp of air. It was what I needed. I got down on my knees, bent my head, folded my hands, and called out to God. After I prayed, I reached for my Bible, and I blew the dust off. When I opened it, my eye went directly to Isaiah 58:11: "And the Lord will continually guide, and satisfy your desire in scorched places, and give strength to your bones. And you will be like a watered garden, and like a spring of water whose waters do not fail."

I look out at my garden. I made it so long ago, when DJ and I started dating, and like my relationship, I had big plans for it. In it I would grow the most delicious vegetables in all of Sack City. Pops and I spent a whole weekend building a fence around it to protect it from critters. I loved putting my hands in the dirt, planting, watering, weeding. And Pops couldn't leave the garden alone either. He'd work in it day after day, even when he wasn't feeling good. In its heyday, Mr. Oakes would buy tomatoes from my garden and sell them at the grocery store. He used to say, "Lynette, your little garden might just be the best in Sack City! Those tomatoes are the most beautiful I've seen!" The fruit grew so big, and the plants rose so tall, they had no choice but to bend in the summer sun. Pops was so proud.

I buried my angel baby in that garden, with a tulip bulb that reveals its bright, beautiful bud every spring without fail. It never lets me forget that a piece of my heart has taken root there. But today I look at the garden outside my bedroom window, and all I see is years of neglect. I am staring at a life that could have been. And it makes my heart heavy. I neglected so many things after DJ left, when Velvet was just a baby. I thought I'd lost the love of my life. Now I see that true love, the kind that comes only from God, has been right here in front of me along. I see that what I really lost was time. And the truth of those days, months, years wasted is bearing down on my soul. If I had reached out to God sooner, Velvet would have had a better mother, Ditty and Pops wouldn't have lost their daughter, my heart would have found love.

I am here now, Lord, and I am ready. I feel the song you've placed in my heart: "Amazing Grace, how sweet

*the sound that saved a wretch like me. I once was lost,
but now am found, was blind but now I see."*

*Today, I will shake this bed loose and return to my
garden bed. I will put on my gardening clothes, walk out
the door and let the sun lead me straight to the broken
gate. I'll take hold of the rake that's worn smooth from
Pops' loving hands, and I will use my hands, God's
hands, to clear a path. I will remove the withered plants
and sprouting weeds. I will cultivate the soil and plant
new seeds. I will make amends and I'll pray—to lower
my pride, to own my mistakes, to stop making excuses,
to listen to my family and give them time to heal. The
task in front of me feels enormous. But God is giving
me strength, renewing a spring in me, and I am finally
ready."*

More neighbors stop by to drop off food and flowers. They
linger, watching Mama work, and try to talk to her, but she's too
focused. So I step in and take their gifts and condolences. All
day, I hum "Amazing Grace" and watch Mama in the garden. I
don't want to miss any part of her coming back to life. All I can
think is, don't stop, Mama. Please don't stop. Even when I pee, I
look out the bathroom window, and pray on the toilet. *Lord, keep
this desire burning in Mama. I'll help any way I can. I promise.*

In the heat of the day, the Lord sends some clouds to keep
Mama from shriveling up in the sun, and I look around with
eyes that see the future for the first time. I was bowling with
my daddy just days ago, and now he's gone forever. Mama was
voiceless and paralyzed with pain, and now, like a rainbow after

a nasty storm, she's come back to life. I wish I could know for sure it will all last. That all the pain of her past, our past, will disappear and never return.

When Sam from the hardware store stops by and hands Mama a bag of seeds, she holds them in her hands like they're fragile and worth taking care of.

"You'll want to plant these wildflowers soon, Lynette," he says. "And let me know if the rabbits start to eat any of your new growth. I have a family trick that will keep them away."

Mama rubs the packet with her thumb and puts it in a pocket of her overalls.

"You take care, now, Lynette. I sure am sorry about your loss. Stop by the store when you're ready for more seeds."

Mama nods her head and says, "Thank you, Sam."

Bobby stops by too, and he doesn't ask many questions, which is nice. We sit on the front step with the sides of our sneakers touching and our knees knocking into each other, just like when we were kids. I don't want the feeling to end.

"So," he pauses. "I've missed you at school, Velvet."

I smile. "I've missed you too."

Bobby's presence reminds me he's been here all along—before Diamond Jim died, before Mama was in the garden. He was here when everything started to fall apart. And now he's here while everything feels like it's coming together. Still, as I look at Mama again, it's hard to trust the falling apart part is really over. I offer a silent prayer: *Please, let it be in the past, Lord.*

"How long has she been working like that?"

"A couple of days," I say.

I lean my head on his shoulder and rest my cast on his knee. Bobby leans his head on mine, and we sit together in the shade of the front steps, watching Mama. His grandmother interrupts our knee knocking and calls him to help clean up her backyard.

Before he leaves, he kisses me again on the cheek and hands me a note. "I'll talk to you soon, Velvet."

My stomach does a little flip. It's like tiny dancers are swinging and kicking my insides. I've been so sad about Diamond Jim and so scared about losing Mama. Spending time with Bobby and watching Mama work in the garden make me feel downright joyful. As Bobby walks across the way, I walk over to Mary in the grotto, where she has a full view of Mama in the garden. I sit with my back against hers and scan the cornfields that extend for miles behind our house.

"Can you see her? She's doing it. She's cleaning up her mess," I say. I pick at the grass next to my thighs and let it fall through my fingertips. "She's coming back to life."

I sit quietly with Mary for a few minutes and open Bobby's note:

Dear Velvet,
I am very sorry about your father. I read the obituary in the paper, and he sounds like a pretty cool guy. I bet you have his bowling skills! I'd like to find out. I just wanted to say I'm here for you.

Love,
Bobby

PS: I wouldn't mind kissing you again like we did up on the hill. When you're ready, of course.

I fold the note and try to hide my smile, but it bursts across my face. I get up and touch Mary's head. I get a glimpse of my cast, and it reminds me how far things have come in a short amount of time. Mama stands with the rake propped under her chin, taking a long pause to admire her work. The piles of weeds and leaves and rubbish she's cleared away are as high as the wobbly fence now. Maybe tomorrow she'll let me help her bag them up.

I open the screen door and hear Ditty on the phone, saying, "Uh-huh," and, "OK. 5:30. OK."

"Who was that, Ditty?"

"It was the manager from the bowling alley."

"What did he say?"

"He's having a farewell celebration for your daddy tomorrow. He asked if we'd come and say a few words."

My stomach tightens.

"Do you think Mama can handle that?"

Ditty shrugs. "We'll just have to find out, sweetheart."

She hands me the morning paper, and it's folded over to page eight, the obituaries. There's a small article with the headline, "Sack City Bowling Champion Honored With Memorial at the Strike Zone This Sunday." It reads:

David James 'Diamond Jim' Hickney died May 12 while helping an elderly couple during the severe thunderstorms that rocked Sack City last week. The

storm created winds that gusted up to 58 miles per hour
and dangerous lightning strikes. It was a lightning bolt
straight to the Strike Zone Champ's heart that caused
his death. Mrs. Whittaker witnessed the traumatic
incident and contacted law enforcement. Police alerted
the local ambulance service, which proclaimed Hickney
dead on the scene. He leaves his daughter, Velvet Mary
Underwood, of Sack City. There will be a get-together
in his honor at the Strike Zone this Sunday at 5:30 p.m.
Guests are encouraged to wear bowling shirts and to
spit-shine their cars.

I set the paper down. Ditty sits by me and pulls me into her
arms. "You OK, honey?"

"Yeah, I guess," I say. "Not good or great or terrible—just
somewhere in the middle."

"Well, that's just OK, isn't it?" Ditty says, smiling, and we
sit there together in the middle of OK.

I turn my attention back to Mama and notice neighbors
lingering and hollering, "Good job, Lynette!" and "Godspeed!"
Mrs. Johnson has decided she might as well set a lawn chair
right in her front yard and watch Mama work. Mama doesn't
seem to mind. Mercy and her parents stop by, too, and Mama
pauses to greet them, leaning in for a hug from Mercy's mom.
Mercy runs to see me, and I tell her Mama chose to clean up
the garden. She knows it's an answered prayer and gives me a
squeeze.

"Tomorrow at the bowling alley, they're having a little get-together to honor Diamond Jim. I may say a few words about him. Will you come?"

"Of course. I'll be there. What are you going to say?" she asks, and I shrug.

The sun starts to set, and Mama keeps going. Ditty has been roasting a chicken, and the savory smell seems to make its way to the garden 'cause Mama calls out, "Mama Ditty, that sure smells good! Will you fix me a plate? I'm starving!"

Ditty's face lights up, and she yells back, "Come on inside, then! You've been working hard all day!"

I sit down at the table, and Ditty makes the mashed potatoes Pops used to love, adding a whole stick of butter and a few pinches of salt. She whips them vigorously and dips her finger in to taste them. My stomach grumbles, but I can't tell if I'm hungry or nervous. I'm thinking of what I might say tomorrow about the man I never knew who I now know in a whole new way. Will Mama say something, too? Who else will be there?

Mama leans the rake against the fence, goes to the corner of the garden, and stares at the flowers people have dropped off. I worry the flowers will remind her that Diamond Jim is gone and send her back into her unconscious state. But she smiles at the thoughtful gifts. It feels like the whole town knows her heart. Maybe they have this entire time.

As she leaves the garden, she scrapes the dirt from the soles of her garden boots—bits and pieces of her past that the rain will eventually carry far from here. She leaves the broken garden gate wide open, pauses, and kneels in front of Mary. When she comes inside, Ditty and I act like we haven't been peeking out at her all day, like we've been inside just minding our own business.

"Oh, how was the garden, Mama?" I ask nonchalantly.

Mama sits down in the same chair where she put her garden boots on this morning and grunts as she takes them off.

"It was a ripe ol' mess, I tell you! Tomorrow I'll finish weeding, and later in the week, I'll run to the hardware store to see if Mr. Oakes has more seeds." Then she sniffs and says, "Mmm, Ditty, you know I love your roast chicken." Ditty smiles. "I'm gonna take a shower before we eat, 'cause my stink is real bad. I forgot how the body responds to a little hard work." Mama scrunches up her nose like she smells.

Ditty says, "You said it, not me," and we all laugh, 'cause Mama does stink something fierce.

Mama walks toward the bathroom, and I remember I left her journal out.

"Mama!" She turns around to see what I need.

"Are you sure you don't want to eat first?"

"Do you see what I look like right now? No, I do not want to eat first."

Ditty looks at me like I've lost my mind and didn't get a whiff of Mama in the kitchen.

"Just make me a big plate, please. I'll be out before you know it."

"You go shower now. We're fine waiting. Aren't we, Velvet?" Ditty nudges me to sit down. I listen for Mama to say something, but nothing happens. No shrieks. Everything sounds normal.

"Velvet, why don't you light the candle on the table?" Ditty asks.

I hear her but I can't stop listening for Mama. My stomach turns. I hear Mama in the shower. Is she actually singing?

"Velvet?" Ditty says again.

I have to tell her. "Ditty?"

"What is it, Velvet?" she says, holding the bowl of potatoes.

"I've been reading Mama's journal. I know Mama lost a baby. And I know more than I should about my daddy. I wasn't trying to find it. It found me." There. It's out. "And ... well ... I was in her room earlier reading it, and I left it on her bed."

Ditty pauses at the table and says, "I'm glad you know, sweetie. The truth has to get out one way or another. The wrath of your Mama over that journal isn't worth your worries. You've handled far worse over the past few days."

Ditty sets down the bowl of potatoes. I know she's right; I have handled worse. And it feels good to get this secret off my chest.

"Today she wrote about letting go of the past. That's why she was in the garden all day; she was clearing it all away."

"Sometimes the Lord puts a fire under your seat when he's tired of watching you sit on it too long. As awful as it is, it took DJ's dying to wake something up in her. Let's be thankful and pray the fire keeps burning."

Ditty sits down at the table, and I fidget in my chair as we wait for Mama.

"Velvet," Ditty sees my nerves are getting to me. "You leave the talking to me."

I barely have time to respond before Mama comes into the kitchen, showered and wearing her favorite robe. She's smiling.

"It sure smells good!"

She doesn't look directly at me, and she doesn't say anything about the journal.

Ditty piles food on Mama's plate, and Mama goes to the cabinet that holds her wine glasses. She opens it, pauses, grabs a water glass and fills it at the kitchen sink.

"Maybe tomorrow I could help you bag up those weeds?" I say.

"Velvet, that's kind, but I want to clean up the garden on my own."

Is it because of the journal? Is she punishing me?

"How about you help me do the planting after it's all cleared out?" she says.

"Sounds great, Mama. I'd love to."

We all enjoy Ditty's supper. Mama is so hungry she wipes up every last drop of gravy with a piece of bread.

"Lynette …" Ditty says as she slides her plate to the side. Oh Lord, here it comes. "There's going to be a special event at the Strike Zone tomorrow evening …" Wait, she's not talking about the journal. "To honor Diamond Jim's passing."

Ditty speaks gently. The room feels as still as it did before the big storm. Mama squirms in her seat.

"The manager, Bill, called. He was hoping that you and Velvet might say something on Diamond Jim's behalf."

Mama grabs a hold of her water glass.

"I'll say something, Mama," I jump in. "So you don't have to."

Mama reaches out to touch my arm. "That'd be nice, Velvet."

She takes a sip of water and sets the glass down gently on the table. Ditty wipes her hands on her apron like her work is done.

"He was real nice, Mama. We had a real nice time," I say.

Mama nods and a tear falls from her eye. "I can see why you fell in love with him."

She reaches for my hand, and I squeeze. I'll hold it as long as she needs me to.

"Ladies," Ditty says, looking at Mama and me, "we have had a few tough days." She gets up, digs in a cabinet, and pulls out a box of Nilla Wafers. "How about if I make us some banana pudding to top off dinner?"

Mama lets go of my hand and smiles. "I can make room for that!"

Just like that, Ditty puts us at ease with the promise of banana pudding. Mama knowing that I read her journal becomes a distant fear. The kitchen window is open, and a gentle wind floats in. I notice Mama's fresh, clean skin. She looks beautiful, peaceful and content.

"In the meantime, let's paint our toenails, Velvet!" Mama says.

"Yes!"

I jump out of my chair to get the polish. On my way to the bathroom, I notice the journal isn't on Mama's bed anymore. She must know. I've been caught. Why didn't she say anything? I sift through the middle drawer of the bathroom vanity and find the bubblegum pink polish that used to be Mama's favorite.

"Want me to paint yours?" I ask Mama.

"Sure! And I'll paint yours," she says.

Ditty doesn't like bubblegum pink, says it would be bad luck at bingo 'cause Louise wears that "God-awful color."

"Velvet and I aren't worried about luck, now, are we?" Mama says.

Mama's feet look pretty. As I paint, she leans back against her chair and hums the tune she was singing in the shower.

"Mama, what's that you're humming?"

"A song I used to sing before I met your daddy."

My spirit hums right along with her.

Ditty can't stand how much fun we're having and gives in. "I guess old Louise won't see my toes inside my shoes," she says, throwing all caution to the wind, and Mama and I cheer.

We eat banana pudding straight out of the casserole dish, and for once Mama doesn't turn on the television.

When we've eaten our fill, Mama stands and puts her hands on my shoulder. "I best be gettin' to bed, ladies. I've got a lot of work to do tomorrow."

"It's going to be beautiful," I say.

I want to remind her tomorrow is also the day we'll officially say goodbye to Diamond Jim at the Strike Zone. I gather courage.

"Don't forget, tomorrow we'll go to the bowling alley ..." I pause.

"Uh-huh," Mama says, mid-yawn.

"We could go to 4 o'clock Mass and walk over after," I suggest. "Maybe Father Matthew will come to the bowling alley and say a few words."

Mama doesn't respond. She squeezes my shoulders tightly, goes to her room and closes the door. Ditty and I stare at each other, wondering what kind of woman will emerge tomorrow.

"I'm going to stay over," Ditty says.

She's not done watching over Mama. I insist she take my bed, but she says she'll sleep on the couch.

On the way to my room, I stand next to Mama's door. Light peeks out from under her door.

Lord, please keep her fire burning. Please keep her heart protected and surround her with your grace and your mercy.

I put on my pajamas and stand in front of my closet mirror. Something looks different. I concentrate on my reflection, trying to figure out what it is, but I can't. I get into bed and pull out my journal. I think about what I'll say tomorrow to honor my daddy. There's so much I don't know about him. Still, I make a list:

He was sincere.
He was a good bowler.
He had a nice car.
He was a hard worker.
He loved my mama and me.

I keep writing the things I do know until the spring breeze blowing gently through my window carries me to sleep.

CHAPTER 27
COMING TOGETHER

I wake to the sound of Mama humming in the garden. It's 6:30 a.m. My notes about Diamond Jim are next to my bed and remind me today is the day.

"Morning, Mama," I call through the window.

Mama looks confused, squinting her eyes at the front door.

"I'm right here, in my room."

"Ha!" Mama turns to me. "Morning, Velvet. It's a good morning to be outside!" She adjusts her sun hat and continues digging in the dirt.

"It is!"

As I walk to the bathroom, I peer into her room. Her bed is made. Her journal is nowhere to be seen. Ditty's in the kitchen, stirring cream into her coffee. The clanking of her spoon reminds me of Pops.

"She's at it again," I say with a grin.

"She sure is." Ditty sips her coffee.

"Pops would have loved it."

"He sure would have. Nothing made him happier than good old-fashioned hard work." Ditty pivots to watch Mama.

"Hey, Mama!" I call out the kitchen window. "How long do you plan on being out there?"

She stops digging briefly. "Until I need to get ready for church and the bowling alley."

Thank you, Lord. She's not going to run and hide. Ditty and I spend the day looking outside, marveling at Mama like we're first timers at the circus and we've got front row seats.

As 4 p.m. approaches, I remind Mama we need to leave for church soon. She takes her time coming in from the garden. As she showers, I put on a dark-colored dress and slip on a pair of Mama's heels. I want to look nice for my daddy. I put Diamond Jim's note in my pocket, so I have a little piece of him near me. Ditty, wearing a black dress and a pretty purple scarf, sits on the living room sofa waiting.

"Well, don't you look all grown up," she says when she sees me.

"Thank you. I feel grown up."

Mama's bedroom door opens. I hold my breath as she walks into the living room wearing a bright red dress and black high heels. Her hair is in a stylish bun, and she smells like jasmine.

"You look so pretty, Mama."

She smiles and grabs her purse.

It's harder than I thought walking in Mama's shoes, but I make it to the truck, and the three of us pile in together. Mama looks at my feet.

"Hot damn, child! You look good in those heels!"

For the first time, I don't even care about apologizing to God for Mama's cursing.

"I feel good in heels!"

"Now I just need to teach you how to walk in them." Mama laughs.

As we pull away from the house, I notice the garden. The freshly tilled soil is free of clutter and full of possibility, just like Mama. We arrive at Our Savior's Bleeding Heart Church, and this time Mama doesn't care about our being the first ones inside. As usual, Father Matthew stands at the door greeting congregants.

"Velvet ... Lynette ... I am so sorry to hear about David James." It sounds weird to hear his real name spoken by Father Matthew like this. "I heard he was a kind, fun-loving man."

Father puts a hand on Mama's shoulder, and she nods and inhales deeply.

"Father," I interrupt. "After Mass, some of us are gathering at the Strike Zone to honor my daddy. I was wondering if you would stop by and say a few words if you have the time?"

"It would be my joy," Father Matthew says, placing his hand on my shoulder.

His touch reminds me of a hug from Pops, and I don't want him to let go.

As we walk toward the front of the church, all heads turn. Bingo Betty makes the sign of the cross as we pass her, the owner of the Suds 'n' Duds smiles warmly, and everyone seems ready to slide down and make room for us. Mama picks the fourth row, and we scooch in and pull the kneeler down together. Mama and I settle in, her red dress draping on the floor, while Ditty mumbles she's too old to kneel. I lay my head on Mama's shoulder, and she rests her head on mine.

We go through all the motions of Mass—the rituals, the

songs, the prayers, the preparation for Holy Communion. I reach into my pocket and touch the note from Diamond Jim, reminding myself what happened. He's gone. *I need you, God.*

As I kneel beside Mama during one of the prayers, it comes to me, what was different when I looked in the mirror last night before bed. I'm no longer the little girl on the swing who didn't know her daddy and who desperately wanted her mama to be happy. I'm a young lady now, able to hear God's melodies in a whole new way. I close my eyes and pray. *Thank you, thank you, thank you.*

After Mass, we file out of church in a slow line while everyone shakes Father Matthew's hand. When we finally get to him, he gathers Mama, Ditty and me close and says, "I'll see you all shortly."

Mama starts the truck and takes out a cigarette.

"Mama, are you gonna smoke at church?" I ask.

"You bet your sweet ass I am."

Ditty mutters, "Lord have mercy."

"Yes, please!" I say and we all laugh.

Mama's cigarette hangs loosely off her lips. I can tell she's nervous, 'cause she fidgets and fusses with her dress. She puts the truck in drive, and we're on our way to say goodbye.

When we pull into the Strike Zone's parking lot, my heart stands still. Diamond Jim's Cadillac is parked at an angle in front of the entrance, spit-shined and gleaming with two red balloons tied to it. I reach over and touch Mama's hand.

Ditty looks the car over and says, "Well, look at that. How nice."

I slide out of the seat and wait for Mama, but she doesn't

move. Her cigarette is still in her mouth, getting shorter by the second. She stares at the car.

"You coming, Mama?" Father Matthew walks toward us. "Mama?"

Her eyes are still fixed on the car. She doesn't seem to see anything else.

I stop Father Matthew before he gets too close. "I think Mama just needs a minute."

"I understand," he says. "How about if I go in and say a few words to the folks inside?'

"That'd be nice. Thank you, Father."

Tired of waiting, Ditty says, "I'm going with him!"

I watch as she disappears into the dark bowling alley with Father, and I'm left alone with Mama and the Cadillac.

I get back in the truck. *Lord? Are you here? I need you.* "How can I help you, Mama?"

Mama pounds her fists on the steering wheel like she's asking it to give her the permission she needs to let go. She releases a cry so deep her voice cracks under its weight. She screams until there's nothing left but breathy attempts. I don't say a word. There's nothing to do but sit by her side and wait.

"I loved him, Velvet," she says, stubbing out her cigarette and putting the butt in the ashtray.

"I know, Mama."

She rubs the tops of her legs, like doing so will give her strength. The constant back and forth makes wrinkles in her pretty dress.

"Mama … I have something to confess."

She reaches for another cigarette and lights it. "I already

know," she says, taking a big drag. "You left my journal on my bed last night, and you've read it?"

She informs and asks at the same time. I nod.

"Part of me is glad 'cause there's so much in there you need to know. But it also makes me sad. A child shouldn't have to read her mother's journal in order to understand her."

"I know about the hurt he caused you and the baby you lost."

Mama lets out a moan and grips the steering wheel.

"I had a dream, remember? About a little boy. I know it seems crazy, but I felt like God was trying to tell me something so I could tell you one day. Your sweet baby is in Heaven!"

I cry as I deliver this news and watch her face. Her features, which were wound so tightly in pain a moment ago, unravel at my words. Mama puts her arm around my shoulder and pulls me closer. The smoke from her cigarette drifts out the window in the direction we need to be heading.

"Diamond Jim was so sorry, Mama. He loved you. And me."

I swallow and hold back my tears, trying to stay strong for her. She takes one more long look at the shiny black Cadillac.

"We can do this, Mama. Together."

Mama reaches for my face and gently squeezes my cheeks. "Yes, we can, Velvet."

Her eyes are softer now. She slides out of the truck, tugs her dress down and pulls her shoulders back. We are ready.

The Strike Zone brims with people, some I know and some I don't. The lights are low, and Diamond Jim's picture has been taken down off the wall of champions and placed on an easel. Candles flicker all around it and make his eyes sparkle like they're magic. I watch, along with everyone else, as Mama walks past their greetings and toward the picture to pay her respects to the man she loved. She reaches out and touches the glass. The noise and talking hush as Mama says her final goodbye. I can't hear what she's saying, and part of me is glad for it. This sacred moment is between her and Diamond Jim. *Please be with her, Lord.* After a few minutes, Mama's dancer friends come to her side and put their arms around her. Mama falls into their kindness.

Mercy and Bobby approach me to say hi.

"How are you holding up, Velvet?" Mercy asks.

"Better now," I say, squeezing her hand.

Bobby says, "He was lucky to have a daughter like you, Velvet," and the way he says it I get the feeling the Lord himself wanted me to know that.

Bill the manager taps me on the shoulder and points to the microphone.

"Whenever you're ready," he says.

"Good luck, Velvet," Mercy and Bobby say in unison.

I see Ditty sitting with Father Matthew, and it makes me smile. Mama heads over to them, accepting hugs from old friends as she makes her way. Mercy joins her family, and Bobby stands next to his grandma, Mrs. Johnson. Mrs. Evans and Janet are here too. I look out at the friends of my daddy, the ones I never got to know. Who was he to them? There's so much I'm thankful for, and so much I want to say about the man I never really knew. I approach the microphone and the room grows quiet. *Lord, I need you.*

"Um, hello." My voice reverberates up and down the bowling lanes. I pull my mouth away from the microphone and smile nervously. "My name is Velvet Underwood. Some of you I know, and some of you I don't, but I'm thankful you're all here."

I hear Ditty cheer, "You're doing great, sweetheart!"

"Because you're all here, that means one of two things. Either you knew my father, Diamond Jim," the words catch on my quivering lip, "or you know and care for Mama and me. And, well, it means a lot to us."

I pause and look at Mama, and she gives me an encouraging smile. "You see, I didn't know my father. Not enough to write something like this for him. I wish I'd known him better. Heck, I wish I could say he was the best father there ever was. That he told me I was pretty, read me my favorite books, rocked me to sleep when I was sick. I wish I could say he taught me how to dance and mow the lawn and skip rocks. That he carried me on his back when my legs got tired. But none of that's true. The truth is, he left Mama and me when I was very young."

People in the crowd look at one another.

"I only recently met him, on the afternoon before he died, right there in lane six." I point, and people turn their heads. "We spent a few wonderful hours together, and he taught me how to bowl." I pause as I remember the grin on his face when he noticed how we both stood in our bowling shoes—heels in, toes out. Tears begin to well up. "I asked him a lot of questions, and he answered them all with an open heart."

Ditty walks toward me and hands me a tissue. "You're doing a fine job, sweetie."

I dab at my eyes. "What I learned is that sometimes people tell a story about themselves. That isn't necessarily a bad thing, unless the story is a lie." My tears fall fast as I think of him parked or standing outside our house on Tender Vine Lane in the dark, unable to come inside to us, his family. "Somewhere along the way, my father started believing the lie that he wasn't good enough for us, that his love was not enough. He left us alone 'cause he thought we'd be better off without him."

Mama begins to cry, and Father Matthew reaches for her hand.

"But I believe forgiveness is for everyone. I believe God held my father in the midst of his lie. And he held Mama and me in the middle of ours too. 'Cause we didn't know, we couldn't know, the lie he'd been telling himself. On the day I met my daddy, he told me he loved me, and he was sorry. And that was the God's honest truth."

I look to lane six and I pause. I move closer to the microphone.

"His name was David James, but everyone called him Diamond Jim. Unless you knew him as my Mama did." I search for her eyes. "He was her DJ."

The crowd smiles and nods and claps. Bill the manager wipes away tears. I go to Mama, who's holding her arms out, waiting for me to fill them.

"He'd be so proud of you, Velvet. I'm so proud of you."

People mingle, and Diamond Jim's friends introduce themselves to me. Many tell me I look like him, which makes Mama laugh. Mrs. Evans asks Mama if she can speak to her, and the two of them go off to a corner and sit for a few minutes. After they talk, Mama hugs Mrs. Evans like a long-lost friend.

"I'm sorry about your loss," Janet tells me, and I hug her 'cause it feels like the right thing to do. And the right thing to do always feels good.

"Maybe we could meet at the pie shop soon," she says.

Mercy's close by, ready to protect me, but quickly realizes Janet means no harm.

"You come too, Mercy," Janet says.

"That sounds nice," Mercy says. "I sure have missed your mama's pie."

The three of us laugh with relief.

Before Bobby leaves, I grab his hand and tell him I read his note. "Thank you for being here for me," I say. "I'd like to go back up on the hill too."

It's dusk when we leave the Strike Zone, and Diamond Jim's car glitters in the sun. Mama doesn't pause to look at it this time. We keep moving forward. We get in the truck, keep the windows down and drive. When we turn onto Tender Vine Lane, we see a bright light in the garden.

"What in the name of Jesus H. Christ is going on?" Mama asks and speeds up.

I decide not to apologize for Mama, I can't save everyone. Her disrespect floats away with the breeze.

When we realize there is a man working in the garden, Ditty grumbles that she's tired of talking to strangers. Mama slows the truck until it stops just short of turning into the driveway and shines the headlights on the mystery man. It's Mr. Sullivan, fixing the broken gate. He stands and waves.

"Ladies," Mama smiles and looks at Ditty and me. "That there is a decent man, a fine man, and I deserve every little bit of his goodness."

"Yes! You do!" we say.

"All this time, he's been right under my nose," Mama says.

"And like the fool that I am, I've been too blind to see it." She pulls down the rearview mirror, lets her bun loose, and focuses on her eyes. "It's about time I start seeing him for exactly who he is."

She tilts the mirror back into position, takes off her shoes, and walks barefoot toward Mr. Sullivan while Ditty and I sit in the truck holding hands. We crane our necks to see what happens next.

Mr. Sullivan swings open the newly repaired gate and reaches for Mama's hand. When Mama grabs hold of his, he pulls her in tight, and I see the back of her hair swaying from side to side against her dress.

"Your Pops sure would like to see this, wouldn't he, Velvet?"

"Yes, he would."

"He fixed the raggedy old fence! If Pops had done it, it'd still be a little bit off," Ditty says, and I double over laughing 'cause she's right. "You know what Pops would have loved most?"

"What?" I ask.

"That he did all that for her, for your mama. It's funny how God works, isn't it?"

"What do you mean?"

"Well, it's like what that nice preacher man always says."

"Father Matthew." I giggle.

"Yes. He says that God's timing is perfect. By the looks of that handsome man in the garden with your mama, he knows what he's doing."

"Yes, he does," I say and pause. "Ditty, remember when you said God wasn't just in churches, that he's everywhere?"

"Yep," she says with satisfaction.

"I believe it now more than ever."

Mr. Sullivan and Mama hold on to each other like they're a trellis that's waiting for moon flowers to sprout and climb up them. All I can think is only God can make this kind of beautiful. Ditty and I slip out of the truck and head into the house so Mama and Mr. Sullivan can enjoy their time alone.

"I don't believe I need to stay here tonight," Ditty says. "By the looks of it, your Mama is gonna be OK."

"Mama is going to be just fine," I say. "And so am I."

"I want you to know how proud I am of you, Velvet Mary Underwood," Ditty tears up.

"Thank you, Ditty. That means an awful lot."

"Your Pops would be real proud of you too." She leans in and kisses me on the nose, just like he used to.

Alone in my room, I take off Mama's borrowed high heels, pull Diamond Jim's note out of my pocket and kiss it. I put it back in the green envelope and add it to the stack of cards from him. I tie them up with the ribbon and hold them to my chest.

I start my routine of getting ready for bed, but nothing feels the same. I'm moving around the same old room but breathing brand-new air. My heart considers for a moment that Mama is more than my mother, Diamond Jim is more than my father, and the people of Sack City are more than my neighbors. With peace in my soul, I close my eyes and feel the holy in everything.

ACKNOWLEDGMENTS

I was a 20-something mom sitting at my antique pine desk (my first big girl purchase) when Velvet came to life. She sprung from my fingertips with the words "I was conceived in the back of a Cadillac, which was smothered in a rich red velvet interior." I remember pulling my hands away from the keyboard, shocked at what had come out. I read it aloud and, as a Midwesterner through and through, further surprised myself by the Southern accent that flowed effortlessly off my tongue. Velvet was eager to be known, and I was happy to set her free.

Over the years, I raised four babies, kept a house, and Velvet continued to pull at my heart. I dabbled here and there with storytelling but ultimately put my writing in the back seat of my minivan (more like the trunk, buried beneath stinky hockey bags and equestrian gear) while I managed an active family.

In my late 40s, I traded the minivan in (the kids could drive their own stinky gear around) and began exploring opportunities to live more creatively. I joined The Twin Cities Writing Studio (the BEST decision I ever made), and though my proclamation scared me half to death, it also filled a gaping void that had been missing for a long time. My commitment to writing bore a great witness to my heart coming to life alongside Velvet's—together we kept our promise.

Velvet is dedicated first to my grandmother, Dorothy, whom we lovingly called Baba. She lived a simple life and spent a lot of time at her kitchen table creating crafts with her hands. When asked why she didn't go to church with Papa, she replied, "Sweetie, I believe God is right here at this kitchen table." And because of that, I did too.

My dear mother, Ruth, you called me a writer before I believed it for myself. Thank you, Mama, for falling in love with Velvet first, for your encouragement and support, and for always believing in my ability to create something special.

To my proud veteran dad, JT, thank you for reminding me after Baba passed away that love is a verb—always.

To my sister, Holly, who has always known, and my brother, Jon, who shows me daily through his creative gifts, that having talent is worth working hard for.

To Peter Laird, a forever thank you for continually guiding my heart in the direction of God's grace. Your teachings are the whisper of my heart allowing me always to see the big picture of life.

I'd be remiss not to share my gratitude for Jennifer Louden, whose writing retreats reminded me that Velvet deserves a seat at the table.

Thank you to my amazing writing teachers at ModernWell, Julie Burton and Nina Badzin, who gave me the confidence to produce my heart's deepest desire. I'll be forever indebted to and grateful for the support and encouragement of my writing group, "The Thursday Girls." Your sweet faces around our oval table helped prompt, shape, and move me across the finish line. I know for sure without you all, this book would still be floating around as short stories filling up space on a cloud somewhere far, far away. Thank you, my dear friends!

To Annie Tucker, without whom I wouldn't be writing this acknowledgment in the back of an actual book. You called me a champion, told me Velvet was unique, and cared for the characters in Sack City as if they were your own. Your words of encouragement strengthened my writing, and I will be forever grateful for your guidance.

To Judy, my mother-in-law, first writing mentor, and forever spiritual hero, thank you for loving Velvet and always believing in me.

A megaphone thanks to my biggest cheerleader and daughter-in-law, Starr! Starr, you make me believe I can do anything!

With my whole heart, I thank my husband, Jay, who taught me the true power of forgiveness. Thank you for listening to me read in a Southern accent for countless hours, always with a loving ear and a soft smile across your face. Your "So good, baby" kept me going all this time.

Finally, it is with tremendous pride that I share Velvet with my most significant accomplishments and four favorite beating hearts: Emmie, Jack, Miles and Ruby. I pray through Velvet you'll always have a piece of me, and if you ever find yourself far from God, you'll close your eyes as Velvet does and see the holy in everything. Look what Mama made!

ABOUT THE AUTHOR

Heather Strommen is a straight-from-the-heart storyteller with a passion for words, characters and storied design. Her debut coming-of-age novel, "Velvet," began as a whisper, the characters dancing in and out of quiet moments, nudging at Heather to bring them to life. Her essays "Wake Up Call," "Making Christmas Perfect" and "The Lies Anxiety Told" highlight the humor and heartbreak of family and were featured at acclaimed Listen to Your Mother live storytelling events. Also the founder of the popular blog and Instagram account, Sweet Shady Lane (@sweetshadylane), Heather is forever designing and refining the world around her and helping others build their own storied design.

Heather is married to her high school sweetheart and lives in Minnesota in a house they lovingly call Little Oak. She and her husband refer to their four adult children as "our best friends."